PROTOCOLS
in the
CLASSROOM

PROTOCOLS
in the
CLASSROOM

Tools to Help Students Read, Write, Think, & Collaborate

David Allen • Tina Blythe • Alan Dichter • Terra Lynch

Foreword by Joseph P. McDonald

TEACHERS COLLEGE PRESS

TEACHERS COLLEGE | COLUMBIA UNIVERSITY
NEW YORK AND LONDON

Published by Teachers College Press, 1234 Amsterdam Avenue, New York, NY 10027

Library of Congress Cataloging-in-Publication Data is available at loc.gov

ISBN 978-0-8077-5904-2 (paper)
ISBN 978-0-8077-7642-1 (ebook)

Printed on acid-free paper
Manufactured in the United States of America

25 24 23 22 21 20 19 18   8 7 6 5 4 3 2 1

Contents

PART II: THE PROTOCOLS

Reflecting on Styles, Preferences, and Expectations

Exploring Questions

PART III: GETTING BETTER WITH PROTOCOLS

Foreword

If you are a teacher and you're ready, this book will grab you. By *teacher*, I mean any subject, any level, any context. By *ready*, I mean that you've discovered viscerally (not just intellectually) that teaching isn't just talking and asking questions, that it depends on real engagement with hard tasks, struggles against the probability of resistance, and *somehow* manages to open unique learning paths for every student. In other words, it's damn difficult, though nonetheless possible—happily so for the sake of the human condition. Maybe you're a teacher working to reach a point in your craft knowledge where the *somehow* of teaching becomes more transparent. Maybe you're trying to balance your listening with your talking. Maybe you're experimenting more in unplanned questions and unexpected answers. Maybe you've taught yourself to pause to allow your students to think, write, display, or talk with each other. If so, you're ripe for the grab. It will come not too far into your reading: You may find yourself suddenly thinking, "I'm going to try this tomorrow." You'll then join a growing group of other teachers who have seized on the word "protocol" from other worlds—technology, science, diplomacy—to signify a unique pedagogy. Drawn from adult learning contexts, it is increasingly evident in other contexts too, especially schools.

Books that presume to help teachers teach well often oversell themselves—but not this one. Protocol pedagogy is not a panacea for problems of disengagement in learning or ineffectiveness in teaching (whether from too much control or too little). Its authors are clear on this point. However, they are also clear that it deserves a place in your practice. And while they eschew jargon and make no claims of a secret sauce, they invite you to try this pedagogy. Very gently, they reveal its provenance, its characteristics, its patterns. They offer simple protocols to try first, then they move on to more complex ones. They coach you through the complexity. Of course, as they note, there are complications and challenges in teaching this way. Hey, this is about learning, after all! But their approach will persuade you to take the risk.

And the payoff, I predict, will be that your students' learning—not just the fruits of it but the processes of it—will become more visible to you than ever before. More importantly, it will become more visible to the students themselves, more available to them for metacognition, more available for agency.

Now before I start overselling the book myself, let me add just two other points of enticement to whatever enticement brought you to the book in the first place and whatever enticement my comments above may have added: the enticements of experiencing the "grab" and expecting a big "payoff."

First, these authors really know what they are writing about—not just protocols (though they are world experts there) but teaching and learning. Their deep knowledge of teaching and learning comes first from their own experience as superb teachers (I don't use this word lightly, and I base my claim on having watched all four of them teach—two as teachers of young people and all as teachers of adults). It comes also from their histories of closely studying teaching and their collective habit of thinking about teaching and learning in fresh ways. Yet they do not depend in this book on just their own experiences. They add the experiences and perspectives of an extraordinary collection of teachers they have interviewed—people who do daily what the book describes.

Second, this book goes way beyond a teaching guide—though it is also a powerful teaching guide. In Part III, it fans out to describe a culture of protocol use available for learning throughout a school's community. And it links protocol pedagogy to other pedagogies focused on discussion—ones you'll also want for your practice, ones that collectively can help us all bury the idea that teaching is mostly talking and asking questions.

—Joseph P. McDonald,
emeritus professor of teaching and learning, New York University

Acknowledgments

Many, many people contributed to the making of this book. We begin by thanking the teachers who opened their classroom doors and shared their stories of using protocols with their students, as described in the chapters in Part II: Barbara Anderson, Christopher Barley, Carole Colburn, Cynthia Elkins, Crystal Fresco Gifford, Beth Hansen, Jaclyn Mann, Caitlin McDermott, Josán Perales, Kristen Schaefer, Charles Shryock, and Daniel Velez.

Other educators who shared their experiences using protocols with students include Jodi Bossio Smith, Michael Eppolito, Luke Freeman, Steve Goodman, David Heroy, Jennifer Krumpus, Peter Lapre, Tamara Parks, Emma Rossi, Gillian Smith, Seth W. Smith, and Alexis Stubbe.

Colleagues and friends who have contributed to our thinking and practice include Ron Berger, Flossie Chua, Anthony Conelli, Kevin Fahey, Beth Graham, Frances Hensley, Beth McDonald, Joseph McDonald, Nancy Mohr, Vivian Orlen, Suzanne Ort, David Perkins, Rosa Pietanza, Ron Ritchhart, Carmen Robles, Jessica Ross, Marlene Roy, Joseph Schmidt, Steve Seidel, Steven Strull, Gene Thompson-Grove, and Shari Tishman.

We are grateful to all our colleagues at the School Reform Initiative, who have provided resources on using protocols to so many teachers and other educators. In particular we thank Kari Thierer and Heidi Vosekas.

Finally, we thank our editors at Teachers College Press: Brian Ellerbeck, Peter Sclafani, Karl Nyberg, and Carole Saltz.

Introduction

The authors of this book—individually, together, and with other colleagues—have for years worked with groups of teachers in using discussion protocols to support teachers' professional learning. Our work has taken place in schools, professional development workshops and institutes, conferences, and university classrooms. Whenever we do this work, one or more of the teachers in the group will say, "I use something exactly like this with my students . . ." or "I am going try this protocol with my kids . . ."

We have written extensively about the use of protocols to support *teachers'* professional learning, in books including *The Power of Protocols, Looking Together at Student Work,* and *The Facilitator's Book of Questions* (see the Resources section at the end of the book). Here, we focus on how teachers use some of the same protocols described in those books to support their *students'* learning. To do so, we draw on our own experiences working with schools and teachers and, more importantly, on the experiences of many teachers who have shared with us their stories of using protocols with their students.

In this introductory chapter, we consider these questions:

- What is a protocol?
- Why use protocols with students?
- How is this book organized?
- How might you use this book?

WHAT IS A PROTOCOL?

Protocols are pervasive in daily life. Some are unspoken, such as the protocol for giving up your seat on a bus or subway to an older person or a person using a cane. Others are more explicit and formalized, such as the set of questions a doctor asks a patient who shows up with a cough or a stomachache. Protocols guide diplomats from different countries and cultures in greeting and conversing with each other, and protocols determine how different computer systems work together productively.

For the purposes of this book, a protocol is simply a way to structure a discussion so that it supports the learning of all participants. Usually the discussions take place orally, but some may be conducted through writing, for example, in a Chalk Talk protocol (Chapter 7) or a Gallery Walk protocol (Chapter 12). The protocols described in this book share four core features:

- A clear purpose that is made explicit for all participants
- An established sequence of steps
- A focus on supporting a group's collaborative thinking and learning as well as the thinking and learning of the individuals within the group
- The cultivation of habits of thinking and learning that are useful in contexts beyond the protocol itself

Clear Purpose

Many people have had the experience of taking part in a lively and interesting discussion only to find later that they were hard pressed to say what its purpose or outcome had been. Protocols, by definition, make the purpose for a discussion transparent to the entire group—without sacrificing the liveliness and interest. That purpose is recognized by the entire group from the very beginning of the discussion through to its completion, which, in protocols, generally includes a reflection on how the discussion achieved its purpose—and how it might do so more effectively.

Some of the common purposes for protocols include:

- Entering and engaging with texts of different types (for example, Save the Last Word for Me, Chapter 10)
- Sharing perspectives on a question, issue, or topic (for example, the Microlab, Chapter 6)
- Giving and getting feedback on a work-in-progress (for example, the Ladder of Feedback, Chapter 13)
- Exploring one's own learning style and expectations for a group's work (for example, Compass Points, Chapter 4)

In Chapter 1, we describe the purposes for each of the protocols in the book and offer suggestions for selecting a protocol that meets the goals you have for your students.

Steps and Sequence

To achieve its specific purposes, each protocol is composed of a set of steps that build upon one another to promote a disciplined thinking process for individual participants and for the entire group. For example, the main purpose of the Tuning Protocol (Chapter 14) is to help a group provide informed feedback on a work-in-progress. It begins with one student (or a team of students) presenting a piece of work (an essay, an outline, a project, a model, etc.) and providing some context for it (including what the presenter[s] wanted to accomplish, what she [or they] would like feedback on, etc.). This step is followed by clarifying questions from the group, which is followed by a close examination of the student work sample(s), which in turn is followed by "warm" (affirming) and "cool" (more challenging) feedback for the presenter. Each step involves a specific kind of thinking and provides a foundation for the steps that follow. For example, the presentation and the clarifying questions provide students in the group with the important context they need to develop relevant and useful feedback.

Group and Individual Learning

Protocols foster the learning of the group, as well as that of the individuals in it. They do so through establishing a shared sense of purpose and a commitment to including all participants' perspectives. Even in a protocol such as the Tuning Protocol described previously, whose purpose is to provide feedback to (typically) just one student on her work, the goal is always to challenge and support the entire group's thinking and learning.

Other protocols, such as Compass Points (Chapter 4) and Three Levels of Text (Chapter 11), ask everyone in the group to respond to the same prompts or to a common text. In doing so, the group builds a deeper *collective* understanding of the issue or the text being discussed. Because protocols emphasize group learning, the omnipresent "debrief" step asks individuals to reflect not only on their own individual experience of the protocol but also on the group's shared experience.

Habits of Mind

Protocols give students the chance to practice the habits of mind that generate powerful thinking and learning. Some of the habits of mind, as described by Arthur Costa and Bena Kallick (Costa, 2008), that protocols emphasize are listening with understanding and empathy, questioning and problem posing, thinking and communicating with clarity and precision, clarifying one's thinking and presentation, remaining open to continuous learning, and managing impulsivity. These are the competencies and skills that teachers hope their students develop and carry with them into college, the workplace, and the larger society in which they participate.

Exercising these habits contributes to a purposeful, engaging, and substantive discussion for all participants. Just as importantly, students can transfer the habits practiced in one protocol to other contexts—not only other protocols but also class discussions and group work of many kinds, as well as individual reading, writing, problem solving, and research.

WHY USE PROTOCOLS?

Using protocols with students is supported by an expanding research literature that demonstrates how students learn through various forms of dialogue, discussion, and debate (for example, Resnick, Asterhan, & Clarke, 2015; Wells & Arauz, 2006; Zwiers & Crawford, 2011). Equally importantly, the use of protocols is validated through teachers' day-to-day observations of the students within their classrooms. In this section, we highlight key reasons for using protocols and also share some observations from teachers.

Building an Instructional Repertoire

Teachers can draw upon protocols' flexibility to help students achieve important learning objectives and standards. Protocols allow teachers to address specific learning objectives and curriculum content by providing students with opportunities to engage actively with that content. For example, the Microlab (Chapter 6) can be used to help students dig more deeply into the core concepts of a science class. Save the Last Word for Me (Chapter 10) can give students the chance to articulate their own interpretations of a primary source and to build on their peers' interpretations. (In Chapter 1, we offer suggestions for matching learning objectives to the protocols included in the book.)

Developing 21st-Century Skills

Sometimes framed as "the four C's"—collaboration, communication, critical thinking, and creativity—these skills are increasingly recognized as essential for success in school, college, the workplace, and society. Such skills are the stock-in-trade of protocols, which push students to articulate their thinking, listen carefully to the ideas of others, and work collaboratively to address key questions and challenges. They foster students' understanding of key aspects of collaboration, such as presenting their work to their peers, asking thoughtful questions of others, providing feedback to one another, etc. Protocols also give students the opportunity to cultivate their own facilitation skills—an essential element of leadership. As Emily Rossi, an English teacher at East Hartford High School in Connecticut, observes, "Once students are familiar with the protocol, they feel confident about how to run the discussion, which frees them up to be bold in what they choose to contribute."

Creating Authentic Opportunities to Assess Student Learning

Because protocols require students to articulate their thinking and understanding of important content, they are rich in opportunities for both students and teachers to observe and document students' learning. Protocols become particularly powerful as assessment tools when used in conjunction with other techniques such as rubrics and students' written or oral self-reflection.

Supporting Focused, Purposeful, and Inclusive Discussion

Protocols provide teachers and students with clear purposes for their collaborative work and a structure to keep the group's discussion focused in relation to those purposes. This is especially important in contexts in which the learning is focused not just on acquiring information but also on grappling with complex concepts that require thoughtful discussion. Open-ended conversation, especially with students who have little experience with it, can feel unfocused or "all over the map." Sometimes a few vocal students dominate while others sit quietly through the whole thing. Protocols "get everyone's voice in the room," says Cynthia Elkins, an arts instructional specialist at Eagle Rock School in Estes Park, Colorado.

Nurturing a Positive Classroom Learning Environment

Protocols provide students with safe and supportive spaces to find their own voice in the classroom—as thinkers, writers, speakers, collaborators, critics, and creators. While protocols may not prevent all

disruptions (as if anything could!), the clarity they provide about purposes, steps, and roles helps students become engaged in and focused
on the work. Students respond positively to discussions in which their
own perspectives are heard and respected, and in which each participant responds thoughtfully and respectfully to others in the group.
Working together in these ways increases trust among students and
improves the classroom learning environment for everyone. Michael
Eppolito, curriculum coordinator for Two Rivers Supervisory Union
in Ludlow, Vermont, puts it this way: "Protocols allow students safe
spaces to try out ideas, challenge each other in respectful ways, and
play different roles in a conversation."

HOW IS THIS BOOK ORGANIZED?

Part I, "Getting Going with Protocols," provides an introduction—
or refresher course—in the use of protocols with students. In this
Introduction, we have defined protocols and considered some of the
reasons teachers use them. Chapter 1 offers guidance and resources
for choosing the right protocol for your goals and the needs of your
students. Chapter 2 addresses key practices for effectively facilitating
protocols, whether you or your students do the facilitation. Chapter 3
describes brief and flexible activities that are useful in preparing students for the kinds of discussions protocols entail. Part I also includes
two additional resources:

- Figure 1.1: Protocol Features summarizes key features of the
  protocols included in Part II
- Figure 2.1: Introducing and Using Protocols includes tips for
  helping your students get started with protocols

These figures are located at the ends of their respective chapters.
    In Part II, "The Protocols," we describe 11 well-known protocols,
organized by four larger categories according to their purposes:

- Reflecting on styles, preferences, and expectations (Chapters
  4–5)
- Exploring questions (Chapters 6–8)
- Entering and engaging with texts (Chapters 9–12)
- Giving and receiving feedback (Chapters 13–14)

Each protocol has proven effective in supporting learning discussions among groups of students within the classroom. For each protocol, we provide an introduction, a detailed set of steps, and tips for using the protocol with students. We also include a brief story from a teacher's classroom illustrating how students engaged in the protocol, as well as the teacher's reflections on its use. These sections provide images of how teachers adapt individual protocols—and sometimes combine different protocols—to support their goals and their students' needs.

The protocols in this book have been developed by individual educators, by groups, and by organizations. Wherever possible, we have recognized the author or authors of the protocols in the book. We have revised the language of the protocol steps, making these more student-friendly; for example, in protocols in which steps are simply numbered, we have added names for each step for easy reference before, during, and after the protocol. The Resources section lists books and websites that provide both more information on individual protocols (and related strategies).

In Part III, "Getting Better with Protocols," we consider some crucial aspects of using protocols effectively with students. These include:

- Getting the most out of the debrief at the end of the protocol (Chapter 15)
- Documenting and deepening learning both during and after a protocol (Chapter 16)
- Troubleshooting challenges that may arise as students learn to use protocols (Chapter 17)
- Understanding how protocols relate to other pedagogical strategies and techniques (Chapter 18)

We conclude the book with some ideas about how you can move from using protocols with students to implementing them with colleagues in order to create or deepen a culture of discussion and inquiry within the school, one that embraces classroom practice and teachers' professional learning. The book also includes a list of Resources for learning more about protocols and related topics.

HOW MIGHT YOU USE THIS BOOK?

We developed this book with classroom teachers in mind. Every teacher's professional knowledge, experience, and context are unique. For teachers new to protocols, we suggest reading the chapters in Part I and perhaps trying out some of the activities in Chapter 3 before jumping into a protocol with students. Figure 2.1 provides a quick-and-easy reference for early uses of protocols with students.

Teachers already familiar with one or more of the protocols in the book, either from their own professional development or from using them with students, may want to consult Chapter 1, "Choosing a Protocol," as well as Figure 1.1, and then peruse the protocols in Part II to identify specific protocols to try. Once you have gained a reasonable comfort level with using protocols with students, the chapters in Part III provide resources for deepening and expanding your work with protocols.

As you introduce your students to protocols, you may find that you take on the facilitator role much of the time. However, protocols offer rich opportunities for students to develop their own leadership skills—as facilitators for, as well as participants in, protocols. For each protocol in Part II, we include a set of steps and facilitation tips that can be shared with students (in some cases, especially for younger students, you may need to modify the language). Of course, as with any complex activity, your modeling will be essential in helping students to become facilitators for one another's learning.

We also hope this book is useful to teachers who want to work with their colleagues to reflect on and improve instructional practice. Such teacher groups might use individual chapters as the basis for a text-based discussion, perhaps using a protocol such as Save the Last Word for Me (Chapter 10) or the Text Rendering Experience (Chapter 9) to guide their conversation. A group might draw on Chapter 1 and Figure 1.1 as the basis for a conversation about matching protocols to their purposes. Larger groups might use a jigsaw technique to break into smaller groups to learn about different protocols in Part II, then share their findings and questions with colleagues in the larger group.

As we hope this book makes clear, protocols are serious tools for supporting learning. They offer opportunities to explore ideas and share perspectives. They are also fundamentally social, meant to support genuine human interaction, with all the warmth, humor, unexpected insights, and occasional digressions that make discussions powerful, memorable, and unpredictable. Have fun experimenting with them—and encourage your students to do so as well!

GETTING GOING WITH PROTOCOLS

CHAPTER 1

Choosing a Protocol

In this book, we describe 11 protocols especially useful for the class-room, as well as a range of briefer protocol-compatible activities (see Chapter 3). These protocols and related activities represent only a small fraction of what is available. For example, the School Reform Initiative website includes over 200 protocols organized into eight categories, of which 14 are specifically designated as protocols for youth engagement (see Resources).

With so many protocols to choose from, how do teachers decide which ones are right for their students, classroom, and curriculum? In this section, we offer some guiding questions for making thoughtful choices.

- How well do your students know each other?
- How familiar are your students with protocols?
- What are your learning objectives for students?
- What habits do you want your students to develop?
- What are your students' strengths and needs?
- How much time do you have with your students?

Figure 1.1, which appears at the end of this chapter, summarizes some of these considerations.

HOW WELL DO YOUR STUDENTS KNOW ONE ANOTHER?

Protocols provide a great way for students to get to know each other and to learn to appreciate one another's perspectives. These are essential ingredients for a trusting, collaborative classroom environment at any point in time but especially at the beginning of the school year or whenever a new group begins to work together. Several protocols included in this book work especially well in supporting initial connections among students and fostering conditions for learning together.

Compass Points (Chapter 4), Fears and Hopes (Chapter 5), and the Microlab (Chapter 6) are particularly effective for these purposes, creating an encouraging and safe space to get students talking and listening to one another right away. These protocols don't require any preparation in terms of reading or writing, since the content for these protocols is usually students' own experiences and perspectives on a question or topic. In addition, these protocols allow each student to decide for herself how much (or how little) to share with the group. Chapter 3 includes several activities that can help students develop the habits practiced in these protocols (the Postcards and Connections activities are particularly relevant).

HOW FAMILIAR ARE YOUR STUDENTS WITH PROTOCOLS?

Another consideration in choosing a protocol is simply students' experience with protocols as instructional tools or strategies. If some or most students are unfamiliar with protocols, it may be helpful to begin with protocols that are somewhat less complex in terms of preparation, roles, and steps.

Some especially good "beginner" protocols are Compass Points (Chapter 4), the Microlab (Chapter 6), Chalk Talk (Chapter 7), the Text Rendering Experience (Chapter 9), and the Ladder of Feedback (Chapter 13). The Microlab is particularly helpful to start with because it very clearly features the key elements of all protocols—focusing on a specific purpose, following a disciplined set of steps, practicing broadly applicable habits, and attending to the learning of both the group and the individual. In the Microlab, students are asked to reflect on a question or a topic individually and then to take turns sharing their responses with two or three classmates—without interrupting or being interrupted. The protocol alternates steps of sharing out and silent reflection. The teacher (typically) facilitates, keeping time and reminding students of their role in each step, so that students can focus on thinking, sharing, and listening. When students are more familiar with the protocol, they can take on the roles of facilitator and timekeeper.

When targeting specific curriculum goals and learning objectives, such as those described in the section that follows, there are protocols with different degrees of complexity or cognitive demand from which to choose. For example, in supporting students in providing feedback on one another's writing (or other work-in-progress), the Ladder of Feedback (Chapter 13) is a good beginner protocol; it gives students four very clear categories to guide the feedback they offer to their peer(s). The Tuning Protocol, which has a similar purpose, may be more challenging initially, since it requires students to concentrate their feedback on a focusing question designated by the presenter.

To help students get used to the steps and the habits required for these longer protocols, it may be helpful to begin with some of the "protocol-friendly" activities in Chapter 3, especially Turn & Talk, 3-2-1, and, in preparation for the Tuning Protocol, Warm & Cool.

WHAT ARE YOUR LEARNING OBJECTIVES FOR STUDENTS?

We have categorized the protocols in Part II according to four big purposes:

- Reflecting on styles, preferences, and expectations
- Exploring questions
- Entering and engaging with texts
- Giving and receiving feedback

Each protocol also addresses several more specific purposes (outlined in Figure 1.1). Teachers can map these purposes onto their specific learning objectives for students. For instance, learning objectives related to analyzing or interpreting texts may lead teachers to choose protocols such as the Text Rendering Experience (Chapter 9), Save the Last Word for Me (Chapter 10), and Three Levels of Text (Chapter 11). These protocols support students in reading with a purpose, making inferences, and using evidence from texts to support interpretations. For objectives related to nonprint texts (paintings, photographs, maps, etc.), the Gallery Walk (Chapter 12) provides a made-to-order tool to develop visual literacy skills, including decoding, interpreting, and questioning visual and multimedia texts.

The Microlab (Chapter 6), Chalk Talk (Chapter 7), and Peeling the Onion (Chapter 8) protocols can help to address specific learning objectives such as using evidence, listening actively, building on one another's comments, and more. For objectives that have to do with revising writing or other student-created products (design projects, multimedia presentations, etc.), the Ladder of Feedback (Chapter 13) and the Tuning Protocol (Chapter 14) provide structure and guidance for students to develop and offer informed and useful feedback on one another's work—as well as to practice receiving feedback from peers.

Some objectives may have more to do with metacognitive goals, for example, helping students to identify their own strengths and needs or how they work best in a group. Compass Points (Chapter 4) and Fears and Hopes (Chapter 5) structure discussions that contribute to these important goals.

WHAT HABITS DO YOU WANT STUDENTS TO DEVELOP?

All protocols cultivate habits of mind. These habits include listening to one another, sharing one's ideas and perspective, and reflecting on one's own—and the group's—thinking and learning. However, a protocol may emphasize particular habits (see Figure 1.1). For example, the Microlab (Chapter 6) strongly emphasizes listening. Chalk Talk (Chapter 7) encourages students to use words and drawing to make connections between their ideas and others'. The Gallery Walk (Chapter 12) highlights close observation and description.

Compass Points (Chapter 4) and Fears and Hopes (Chapter 5) provide a safe space to develop the habit of understanding others' ideas and perspectives. Text-oriented protocols, including the Text Rendering Experience (Chapter 9), Save the Last Word for Me (Chapter 10), Three Levels of Text (Chapter 11), and the Gallery Walk (Chapter 12) encourage paying close attention to detail and nuance.

WHAT ARE YOUR STUDENTS' STRENGTHS AND NEEDS?

All protocols in the book can be used with students at all academic levels and across disciplines or subjects. However, some are particularly helpful in differentiating instruction and curriculum content to meet the needs of individual students and groups of students, especially in terms of language development.

Protocols can help language learners and others who may struggle with academic language or with expressing their thoughts verbally or in writing. For these students, the Text Rendering Experience (Chapter 9), Save the Last Word for Me (Chapter 10), and Three Levels of Text (Chapter 11) provide clear purposes for reading a text. They also create space for students to think and reflect before speaking. For example, Save the Last Word for Me (Chapter 10) allows the presenter to listen to others' ideas before offering her own comments.

Many students benefit not only from having time to think but also from being able to visualize how a topic develops in a discussion.

Chalk Talk (Chapter 7) allows students to use writing or drawing to process their ideas and make connections to others' ideas before discussing them orally within the group. The Gallery Walk (Chapter 12) invites students to draw upon and develop their visual literacy as a key component of discussion.

HOW MUCH TIME DO YOU HAVE WITH YOUR STUDENTS?

Time is always an issue in planning for classroom instruction. Inevitably, some protocols take longer than others, especially when multiple small groups are working simultaneously with the same protocol.

Many protocols in the book are extremely flexible and can be completed in as little as 15–20 minutes. These include Fears and Hopes (Chapter 5), the Microlab (Chapter 6), Chalk Talk (Chapter 7), Save the Last Word for Me (Chapter 10), and the Ladder of Feedback (Chapter 13)—though each can also take more time if a sustained discussion is in order. Some protocols, such as Compass Points (Chapter 4), Three Levels of Text (Chapter 11), and the Tuning Protocol (Chapter 14), typically take 30 minutes or longer.

While most protocols can be organized and conducted on an impromptu basis (for example, in response to an emergent question or need), a few protocols, especially the Gallery Walk (Chapter 12) and the Tuning Protocol (Chapter 14), require advance planning and materials preparation.

All protocols gain power when students have ample time to reflect on their learning within the discussion. For this reason, all conclude with a debriefing step. This might be conducted briefly with a 3- or 4-minute go-round within the group. However, when time permits, it is valuable to allow a more extensive debrief, perhaps involving individual written reflections followed by discussion (see Chapter 15: Getting the Most Out of the Debrief).

Teachers consider many other factors in selecting protocols: Should the teacher or the students facilitate? Which type of text works best with which text-based protocol? Which protocol might serve as a lead-in or a follow-up to another protocol or another instructional strategy? These and other considerations will become more apparent once you and your students have some solid experience using the protocols themselves. The next chapter provides some of the "nuts and bolts" information that can help you and your students get started.

Figure 1.1. Protocol Features

Protocol	Purposes	Habits	Notes
Reflecting on styles, preferences, and expectations			
Compass Points (Chapter 4)	To understand individual preferences for group work	Understanding others' ideas and perspectives	Also known as "N-S-E-W"
	To understand how preferences may impact others	Understanding individual differences	A good whole-class protocol
		Self-reflection	Review definitions of each "direction" with students before they choose a direction
Fears and Hopes (Chapter 5)	To learn about one another	Articulating one's ideas and perspective	A good protocol to begin new year or unit
	To develop norms of group ownership and responsibility	Understanding others' ideas and perspectives	The teacher should facilitate until students are comfortable handling potentially sensitive topics
	To bring concerns into the open and begin addressing them collectively	Surfacing differences and uncomfortable feelings	
Exploring questions			
Microlab (Chapter 6)	To address a question so that each member of the group gets a chance to respond	Reflecting on a question	A good protocol to practice listening skills
	To listen to others' perspectives on the question	Articulating one's ideas and perspective	Framing a compelling question that invites multiple perspectives is essential
		Listening	
Chalk Talk (Chapter 7)	To reflect on a question or topic	Articulating one's ideas and perspective	A good protocol for students who may struggle to express themselves orally in a group
	To generate ideas or solve problems	Making connections to others' ideas and perspectives	Requires lots of paper and space to write and draw
	To make thinking visible	Clarifying thoughts, ideas, questions, concepts, etc.	

Figure 1.1. Protocol Features (continued)

Protocol	Purposes	Habits	Notes
Peeling the Onion (Chapter 8)	To explore a problem or dilemma	Articulating one's ideas and perspective Understanding others' ideas and perspectives Resisting the inclination to solve a problem before understanding it	Helpful for teacher to preconference with student(s) presenting the problem or dilemma to help develop a focusing question
Entering and engaging with texts			
Text Rendering Experience (Chapter 9)	To enter a text To collectively make meaning of a text	Reading closely Paying attention to detail and nuance	Usually works best with a relatively short text everyone in the group has read or can read together before the protocol Recording student responses to the text provides good resource for later discussions and writing
Save the Last Word for Me (Chapter 10)	To enter a text To collectively make meaning of a text	Referencing textual evidence Understanding others' ideas and perspectives Synthesizing others' ideas	Similar to Text Rendering Experience, except student presenting text listens to others before sharing her thoughts about it

Figure 1.1. Protocol Features (continued)

Protocol	Purposes	Habits	Notes
Three Levels of Text (Chapter 11)	To deepen understanding of a text To collectively make meaning of a text To explore connections between the text and students' thinking and writing	Articulating one's ideas and perspective Understanding others' ideas and perspectives	Similar to Text Rendering Experience and Save the Last Word for Me, but it encourages students to connect passages from text to their own reading, writing, and thinking
Gallery Walk (Chapter 12)	To encounter, explore, and interpret texts of all kinds To share perspectives on texts with others	Closely observing and describing Articulating one's ideas and perspective Making connections to others' ideas and perspectives	Teacher or teacher and students select and post exhibits prior to protocol In the Hosted Gallery Walk variation, students present exhibits of work they have created
Giving and receiving feedback			
Ladder of Feedback (Chapter 13)	To provide informed and constructive feedback on a work-in-progress To learn about one another's work	Giving balanced, specific feedback Resisting the impulse to leap to judgments or suggestions	Student presenter(s) prepare a brief description about work-in-progress before protocol begins
Tuning Protocol (Chapter 14)	To provide informed and constructive feedback on a work-in-progress To learn about one another's work	Identifying specific evidence Sharing one's ideas and perspective Understanding others' ideas and perspectives	Similar to Ladder of Feedback, but student presenters develop a focusing question to guide feedback Teacher should preconference with student presenter(s) and facilitator(s) before protocol

CHAPTER 2

Facilitating the Protocol

Protocols need thoughtful facilitation in order to be effective. While facilitating protocols is not difficult, a little practice definitely helps. Many teachers serve as the facilitator, especially the first time they introduce a new protocol to students. With a little modeling and coaching, students—even young ones—can take on this role in smaller groups and sometimes even for a whole-class discussion.

The facilitator's job spans four stages:

- Preparing for the protocol
- Introducing the protocol
- Guiding the protocol
- Closing the protocol

In the sections below, we describe key "moves" the facilitator makes at each stage to support the group's thinking and learning. We address the teacher as facilitator directly (and count on *you* to find the best way to share these moves with your student facilitators). We focus here on the essentials of facilitation—the things you will do every time you use a protocol. Since teachers and students have different levels of experience with protocols, Figure 2.1, which appears at the end of this chapter, offers tips for introducing protocols to students for the first time, as well as for introducing a new protocol to experienced protocol users. In Part III, we explore in more detail some of the challenges facilitators encounter as well as strategies for developing facilitation skills and deepening learning in protocols.

1. PREPARING FOR THE PROTOCOL

Preparations for using a protocol usually take place during the day or days before you use the protocol in your classroom. These preparations

include choosing the protocol, reviewing the protocol steps to anticipate challenges and make adaptations for your students, and preparing all required materials. Even after your students have experience
enough to take on the facilitator role, you may still take the lead in
these preparations.

Note: Some protocols, including Fears and Hopes (Chapter 5), the
Microlab (Chapter 6), and the Ladder of Feedback (Chapter 13), require little (or no) advance preparation. These can be integrated into
a lesson on an impromptu basis. This is also true of some protocols
for entering and engaging with texts, including the Text Rendering
Experience (Chapter 9) and Save the Last Word for Me (Chapter 10),
if students already have copies of the text.

Choose the Protocol

Identify the protocol that best fits the learning goals and your students' level of experience and needs. (See Chapter 1 and Figure 1.1 for
guidelines for selecting appropriate protocols.)

Review the Steps of the Protocol

Once you have selected a good protocol for your purposes, review the
steps to anticipate challenges in using it with your students. As you
review the protocol, ask:

- Are any steps likely to be especially tricky for your students?
  How might you prepare students for these? (See Figure 2.1 for
  more preparation strategies.)
- How much time is each step likely to require? How might the
  timing be adjusted to fit the amount of class time available?
  How might it be adjusted to fit your students' current skill
  level? (Will they need more time for some steps? Or perhaps a
  little less?)
- What other adaptations might you need to make to this
  protocol to ensure students achieve the goals? For example,
  what changes should you make to suit students' reading
  abilities? Should the wording be simplified or terms explained
  or modeled (for example, by providing sample phrases or
  sentence stems)?

Make Copies of the Protocol

Once you have made any necessary adjustments and adaptations to the protocol, make copies of it so that every student can follow along while using the protocol in class. Large print and a clear font can make it easier for individual students and the group to refer to it during the discussion. Leaving space on the page for students to take notes may also help.

Identify Presenter(s) and Help Presenter(s) Prepare

In protocols such as the Microlab, Compass Points, Fears and Hopes, the Text Rendering Experience, and others, all participants engage in the same activity, for example, responding to a text or a question. However, some protocols call for presenters to share samples of their own work with the class. Such protocols include the Ladder of Feedback (Chapter 13), the Tuning Protocol (Chapter 14), Peeling the Onion (Chapter 8), and some versions of the Gallery Walk (Chapter 12). For these protocols, the facilitator needs to do some additional pre-protocol work, including:

- *Identify the presenter(s).* This step involves designating a student (or students) ready to present work to the group for feedback. This is usually best done by inviting volunteers but may also involve some active encouragement from you as well. In some cases, teachers create a schedule so that presenters know in advance when their turn to present is coming up.
- *Help the presenter(s) prepare.* Talk with the presenter(s) in advance of the protocol. Describe the protocol, its purpose and steps, and determine with the presenter the kind of work that she will share in the protocol. If the protocol involves the group in giving feedback to the presenter, talk with the presenter about the kind of feedback she wants (and doesn't want).

The protocol-specific chapters in Part II also provide guidance on helping presenters to prepare.

Prepare Materials

In addition to a copy of the protocol for each participant, different protocols require different materials, for example, texts, samples of student work, a carefully framed question or issue for discussion. Give some advance thought to how to make these accessible to participants during the protocol.

- If the focus of the protocol is a text, an object, or an image, consider what kind of room set-up and use of technology will make it easiest for students to engage with such things. For example, if you are displaying an object or showing a video, will everyone be able to see it? Are reproductions of photographs or paintings large enough for students to see? Should there be multiple copies, or should the objects or texts be arranged and displayed on walls or tables?
- If the focus of the protocol is a sample (or samples) of student work, as in the Ladder of Feedback (Chapter 13), the Tuning Protocol (Chapter 14), or the hosted version of the Gallery Walk (Chapter 12), consider how best to reproduce or display the work so that everyone can read or observe it closely.

2. INTRODUCING THE PROTOCOL

Protocols are most effective when, right from the start, everybody involved has a clear idea of the purpose for the protocol, how the steps will play out, and their own roles within the discussion. Here are some helpful moves the facilitator makes to accomplish these tasks.

Explain (or Remind the Group of) the Purpose

It usually takes just a minute or two for the facilitator to share the purpose and check in with participants to make sure everyone understands it. Review the purpose, even if the students have used the protocol before. You can often accomplish this by asking a student to describe the purpose and inviting others to clarify as necessary.

Review Steps of the Protocol

The facilitator should also make sure that every member of the group has a hard copy of the protocol steps (or can easily see the steps on chart paper or a projector). After reviewing the steps verbally, allow time for each member of the group to read through the steps, and then invite any clarifying questions about the process. Encourage students to ask process-related questions at any time during the protocol (for example, about how a particular step is meant to work or what their role is within any step), reminding them that the goal is not to do a perfect protocol but to use the protocol to support thoughtful, focused discussion.

As you review the steps of the protocol, let students know how much time each will take. For all the protocols included in Part II, the times provided serve as a guideline. These times can be modified: Some steps may be extended or condensed to fit the time you have, the size of groups, the length and complexity of a text, and other factors. However, we recommend establishing the times before the protocol begins, sharing these with students, and sticking to them once the protocol is underway.

Review Norms

Norms are the expectations a group has for the spirit in which it wants to conduct a discussion. While the protocol identifies steps that the group follows, the norms help the group understand how to carry out those steps and relate to one another throughout the discussion. While each class may develop its own specific norms for protocol-guided discussion and other activities, here are a few we have learned through our work with other educators that we recommend for any protocol and any group:

- *Offer respect for others' work and thoughts.* Treat the work and the ideas that others share with as much respect as you would want your own work and ideas to be treated.
- *Share the air.* Be aware of how much you are talking; make sure there is plenty of "airtime" for all participants.
- *There is no monopoly on expertise.* Everybody in the group has a perspective to contribute; no one participant's perspective has priority or higher status.

- **_Learning is a team sport._** Participating in a protocol is not a competition for the group's or the teacher's attention or approval.

It can be helpful to have the norms posted in a visible place. This makes it easier for the facilitator, or any member of the group, to refer to them during the protocol itself or in debriefing it.

Make Groups

One of the most important decisions you will make in using protocols is how to group students. You may choose to conduct the protocol as a whole-class large group, with you facilitating. This can be a great way to introduce a protocol, but it limits the opportunities for all students to actively contribute. (To get all students talking in a larger group, you can build in opportunities for Turn & Talk during some steps; see Chapter 3.)

As students become familiar with protocols, it is more effective to organize multiple small groups that all use the same protocol simultaneously. You might continue to play the role of facilitator for all these small groups, announcing next steps and keeping time from the front of the room. However, designating a student facilitator (and possibly a timekeeper and recorder) for each group is often easier. Students playing these roles, as well as students serving as presenters in the groups, should be clear about their responsibilities before the protocol begins. Even when students are facilitating small groups, you still have an important role to play in moving throughout the classroom, observing groups at work, and intervening as necessary to help them refocus.

Another option is to use a fishbowl strategy (Chapter 18), in which some students take part in a protocol while others observe. This can be a good way to learn a protocol, but the ultimate goal should be to get all students actively and fully participating in the protocol.

Assign Roles

Protocols not only structure time and sequence activities but also designate the roles individuals play within the discussion. All protocols have a facilitator. Be clear before beginning who will facilitate—you or one of the students. If it is a student (or multiple students in the case of multiple small groups), make sure each has a good understanding of the role and knows to ask you any questions during the protocol. (You can find more resources to help prepare the facilitator, whether you or a student, in the chapters in Part II that describe individual protocols.) Other roles that might be assigned are a timekeeper and a recorder (or "scribe") to capture ideas (on chart paper, laptop, Smart Board, etc.) that come up during some steps of the protocol.

3. GUIDING THE PROTOCOL

Once the protocol is underway, the facilitator does a few different things to help it stay on track. These moves help the group stay true to the protocol steps, allow for sufficient time for a full discussion, and ensure that everyone has the opportunity to participate in the discussion.

Mark Transitions from Step to Step

Each step of the protocol builds on the previous one and contributes to the learning within the overall discussion. The facilitator helps the group by signaling when one step is coming to an end and then introducing the next step. Especially for students who are learning the protocol, it can be helpful to remind them of the purpose of each step, for example: "Now we're going to move on to the step where we provide warm feedback to the presenter about her work. This step is important because the presenter needs to know what to keep and build on as she revises her work."

Keep Time

Most protocols have suggested time limits assigned to each step. Signal to the group when the time for each step is about to end, for example, "We have one more minute left for clarifying questions." Then help them shift to the next step: "Okay, that's all the time we have for clarifying questions. We probably didn't get to all of them, but that's okay."

Of course, the facilitator may also recognize the need to either add time (just a minute can have an impact on the discussion) or move to the next step before the designated time is up. However, be careful about moving ahead too quickly just because the group is momentarily silent. Allowing the silence to linger for a few extra seconds often makes space for new ideas, questions, or comments to emerge.

Help Participants Stick to the Steps

Protocol-guided discussions require that students think about both what they want to say as well as how and when they should say it. This discipline is challenging for many—students and adults alike—and takes practice. A facilitator's gentle reminder about sticking to the step at hand usually helps refocus individuals and the group. For example, in the Text Rendering Experience (Chapter 9), you might say, "Remember, at this point each person is only sharing a sentence from the text. We'll get to phrases and single words in the upcoming rounds."

Make Sure Everyone Has the Chance to Participate

Protocols only work if everyone feels comfortable sharing their ideas with the group—without feeling forced to do so. If some students have been quiet for several steps, you might try a few moves:

- Encourage students to raise their hands and wait for the facilitator to acknowledge them before they speak. (The facilitator can then make an effort to call on those who have not spoken.)
- If some students have been quiet for several steps, you might try saying, near the end of the next step: "We have two more minutes in this step. Let's leave a space for those who haven't yet participated to make a comment if they'd like to."
- At the beginning of each step, call for a minute of quiet and invite students to make notes about any comments they would like to offer. Sometimes, students just need a moment of quiet to organize their thoughts before they feel comfortable sharing them out loud.
- Include a Turn & Talk (Chapter 3) within a step. Some students may feel more comfortable expressing their ideas with a single classmate than with the entire group. Talking to a partner may help them feel comfortable to share out in the larger group.

These moves will not address all situations that may occur within a protocol. In Chapter 17, we share some other strategies to help foster inclusive and positive participation within the group.

4. CLOSING THE PROTOCOL

Almost every protocol concludes with the same two steps: expressing appreciation for the presenter's role and the debrief.

Thank the Presenter

Not all protocols have a presenter role. For those that do, the facilitator invites the group to thank the presenter(s), usually before the debrief step. This is also a good time for the group to express its appreciation for students who have served as facilitator, timekeeper, recorder, etc.

Debrief the Protocol

Protocols encourage reflection not only on a text, a student work sample, a question, a dilemma, or whatever provides the focus for the discussion, but also on how the group conducted the discussion. The debrief step at the end of the protocol provides the opportunity for everyone to deepen their understanding of the purpose of the protocol, including how and when to use it. It also enables students to reflect on their own skills as collaborators and learners and to appreciate the power of hearing multiple viewpoints on a text, a work sample, or a topic.

Important questions the facilitator might invite students to reflect on during the debrief step include:

- What was it like to use the protocol? What was most helpful about it and why? What did you struggle with and why?
- What could we do next time to make our use of this protocol (or other protocols) a more powerful learning experience for everyone?
- How else could you imagine using this protocol?

In addition, you might invite students to reflect on the role the facilitator played in supporting the discussion. While focusing on the facilitator's role during the debrief may at first feel awkward, especially for student facilitators, discussing specific facilitation moves that supported the group during the protocol is an excellent way to develop everybody's understanding of facilitation.

In Chapter 15, we share additional suggestions for questions that groups might use to reflect on their experience of the protocol. We also share reflections on challenges that might emerge during the debrief and how you might address them.

Figure 2.1. Tips for Introducing and Using Protocols

This resource provides a menu of suggestions for introducing students to the idea of protocols. For students familiar with protocols, it offers ideas for introducing them to new, unfamiliar protocols. Finally, it highlights some important things for students to keep in mind in using protocols.

Tips for Introducing Protocols to Students Who Have Never Used One

- Explain that using protocols can help everyone develop good habits, including active listening, sharing ideas and perspectives, and being open to others' perspectives.
- Use the analogy of a game: Like a game, a protocol has goals. It also has specific "rules" (steps, roles, etc.) that may make the game more challenging but also allow everybody to play in ways that are fair and satisfying.
- Talk about the purpose of the protocol with students. Allow time for students to read the purpose and ask clarifying questions.
- Invite students to develop norms to follow during the protocol. Consider providing initial norms for the group's work (see Chapter 2) and then revise them after the protocol. Using the Fears and Hopes protocol (Chapter 5) first can help students identify norms related to their own concerns and expectations for a new protocol.
- As you move from step to step within the protocol, remind students of the purpose of each step and how much time it will take. Let students know that you will give them a 1–2 minute warning when getting close to the end of a step.
- Remind students that they will have a chance to debrief, or talk about, the protocol afterward and that you are eager to hear their thoughts about it. Then make sure to do that! Turn & Talk, the All-Purpose Go-Round, or 3-2-1 are all useful structures for the debrief (see Chapter 3).

Figure 2.1. Tips for Introducing and Using Protocols (continued)

Tips for Introducing a New Protocol to Students Who Are Familiar with Protocols

- Review the new protocol with students and ask them to compare it with a familiar one: What are the similarities and differences they notice? Point out others that may not be obvious to students.
- If time permits, use Fears and Hopes (Chapter 5) to surface students' expectations for the new protocol.
- Emphasize purpose: Different protocols are structured to achieve different purposes, just as different tools are made to do different tasks. (No one would want to cut the grass with a pair of scissors or trim their hair with a hedge clipper.)
- Remind students that they will get to debrief the new protocol. Tell them you are looking forward to hearing their thoughts about it and how it compares to other protocols they have experienced.
- New protocols often require new steps or moves, for example, clarifying questions, "warm" and "cool" feedback, debriefing. Practice these before a protocol, and provide reminders about their use during the protocol.

Things for Students to Keep in Mind in Using Protocols

- Protocols require practice. They may not all go smoothly the first time— or maybe even the second or third time.
- Not everyone loves protocols or a specific protocol. Some people just prefer to say what they want to say when they want to say it. There is a time and a place for that, just as there is a time and a place for using a protocol to guide the discussion.
- Acknowledge with students that it can be difficult to wait their turn and to do the steps in order. Suggest that they try making notes; that way they can listen to other people and not forget what they want to say.
- Protocols can be confusing at times. Tell students not to be afraid to let the facilitator know if they are not sure about what they should be doing at any point during the discussion.
- Feeling uncomfortable is not necessarily a bad thing. It often signals a learning opportunity.
- Silence is golden. Sometimes a quiet pause can be just what is needed to allow everyone's thinking to go deeper.
- Encourage students not to hold back in the debrief! It is important for them to share their experiences—what they liked, what they did not, questions, "aha moments," etc. This is where much of the learning happens.

CHAPTER 3

Building Buy-In and Practicing Habits

Using protocols to guide discussion can lead students to richer thinking, deeper learning, and stronger personal connections to both the curriculum and to one another. Getting to these important outcomes requires some initial investment of time to help students learn how to use protocols well.

Protocols are thought-demanding exercises, requiring habits of behavior and thinking skills that may pose challenges for students. Some of those habits and skills include:

- Articulating ideas aloud
- Speaking within time constraints
- Staying focused and resisting digressions
- Following a sequence of steps in a disciplined way
- Formulating questions
- Listening attentively
- Understanding others' perspectives

The activities in this chapter help students to develop these kinds of skills and habits. They are typically brief, taking as little as 5 minutes. They can be used in two key ways:

- *As brief, stand-alone exercises.* You can embed these activities throughout the period or school day—perhaps as openers or closers for your lessons, or to address questions or topics that emerge during daily learning in the classroom. This approach can be especially helpful if you feel that your students are not quite ready to engage in a full-fledged protocol. These activities help students to practice protocol skills and develop habits in small, manageable chunks so that when you do introduce them to a full protocol, important aspects of it will already feel familiar to them.

- **As supplemental steps embedded within a protocol.** You might decide to give your students some extra support during a particular step of a protocol by drawing on one or more of these activities while you are engaged in protocol-guided discussion. For example, if you think students might be hesitant to articulate their thoughts during a particular step, you might opt to begin that step by first having students do a Turn & Talk and then inviting them to share their thoughts in the larger group. If you are concerned that some students are getting crowded out of the discussion by other, more assertive talkers, you might decide to use a Go-Round within a step in the protocol, in which all members of the group share a brief response. Similarly, Warm & Cool or 3-2-1 can be used to give more structure to the debriefing step at the end of a protocol.

As these activities help students practice the skills and habits needed for protocols, they also sow the seeds of two other important conditions that enable protocols to operate more successfully in your classroom:

- **Buy-in.** Students are more likely to engage willingly in an exercise or an activity when they understand its purpose and when the skills required by the activity are appropriately challenging. These short activities help students (and teachers) to test the waters of structured discussion. Buy-in generally occurs gradually—after an investment of time and effort that yields results rather than as the result of a great sales pitch. These protocol-friendly activities require only a small investment of time and minimal degree of risk, allowing teachers and students to build habits, practice skills, and gain experience for protocols like those in Part II.
- **A supportive classroom learning environment.** In doing these exercises, students take small steps toward getting to know one another as learners, thinkers, and collaborators. The exercises also create important opportunities for teachers to get to know their students better, revealing students' thinking as well as the ways in which they are (and are not)

comfortable as they take part in structured, collaborative learning. Feeling known within the classroom community is an important step toward developing trust. With greater trust comes the willingness to take risks, share problems, offer critical feedback, and listen attentively—all habits crucial to protocols and effective collaboration.

Note: These activities have existed in many versions with many creators and adapters. In compiling them here, we have drawn on several sources, including *The Power of Protocols*, the School Reform Initiative website, and resources offered by EL Education (formerly known as Expeditionary Learning) and Facing History and Ourselves. See Resources for additional information.

ALL-PURPOSE GO-ROUND

Purpose: Sharing responses to a question and encouraging equitable participation

The facilitator asks the group to reflect on a question. After a minute or so of silent, individual reflection, each participant, going in order, shares their response briefly. The facilitator may designate a certain time limit per person (say, 15–30 seconds) to help students keep their responses brief. No questions, comments, or other responses to individual contributions are permitted during the go-round.

CONNECTIONS

Purpose: Reflecting on how everyone is doing and feeling—as individuals and as a group

After a few minutes for silent reflection on how each participant is feeling, what they are thinking about, etc., the facilitator opens the discussion for anyone who would like to share something. After one person shares, anyone else in the group may make a connection to the first speaker. After that, students may make a connection to any of the previous speakers. No one is required to share; no one should speak more than once. The facilitator decides when it is time to close the discussion. (Developed by Gene Thompson-Grove; see School Reform Initiative website in Resources.)

POSTCARDS

Purpose: Generating ideas for and interest in a topic

This activity requires a set of picture postcards; the best ones to use are those that require some interpretation. The facilitator distributes a postcard to each student, asking that students not look until told to do so. The facilitator then poses a prompt designed to get the students talking about some aspect of the upcoming topic; for example, "The card you have has a picture. How does the picture remind you of your favorite book?" ". . . of a time you were on a school trip?" ". . . of an experience you had working in groups?" Students are given 30 seconds to think of a response (or more for younger students). Then they share in small groups. The facilitator may then ask a few volunteers to share publicly, or, if the class is small enough and time allows, do a go-round in which everybody shares. The facilitator might also have two students share the same card and talk about what was similar and different about their reactions. (Adapted from Postcards from the Edge from the School Reform Initiative website; see Resources.)

3-2-1

Purpose: Taking stock of students' knowledge about and interest in a topic, text, or experience

The facilitator asks students to reflect on and briefly write (perhaps on a card or sticky note) in response to three prompts related to a text, topic, or other learning experience with which they have been engaged: three things you discovered; two things that were interesting to you; and one question you still have. Students then share their responses orally, either in small groups or within the large group. 3-2-1 can be used at the start of a discussion to share prior knowledge and generate questions to explore, as an "exit ticket" to assess learning during the lesson, or at any point in a group's work together. It can also provide a structure for the debrief of a protocol.

TURN & TALK (ALSO KNOWN AS PAIR–SHARE)

Purpose: Sharing perspectives on a question or topic

The facilitator gives the group a simple prompt: "Turn to a partner sitting next to you (or near to you) and talk about. . . ." This may be a question, a topic, a quote, an image, etc. It can be used before the full class engages in an activity related to the question/topic or to discuss a question/topic that has emerged during a protocol or an activity. The facilitator often gives a set time (for example, 2 minutes) and instructs the pairs to "share the air time." The facilitator may choose to ask pairs to share out from their discussion, though this is not required. This activity is also useful when a discussion seems hard to get started, for whatever reason. Asking students to "turn and talk" gives them a chance to practice articulating their thoughts on a small scale before doing so with the entire class.

WARM & COOL

Purpose: Generating feedback on an idea, plan, or work-in-progress

After a summary of the idea, plan, or work-in-progress, the facilitator asks each participant to write down at least one piece of "warm" feedback, that is, something that seems strong or promising about the work, and one piece of "cool" feedback, that is, something that may need development or improvement. In separate rounds for warm and cool, participants share their feedback briefly, while the presenter listens and takes notes but does not respond. (See Chapter 14: Tuning Protocol for more on warm and cool feedback.) This activity is very similar to both Glows & Grows and Wows & Wonders.

Part II

THE PROTOCOLS

CHAPTER 4

Compass Points

Compass Points, also known as N-S-E-W (North-South-East-West), helps students explore their preferences for working with others in groups. While the points on the compass bear some similarity to categories of the Myers-Briggs Personality Inventory, the goal in this protocol is for students to understand how their style of working relates to that of others with whom they collaborate.

Students self-select into a group associated with one of four directions—North, South, East, or West—based on descriptors of each. As a group, they answer questions related to the impact their style has on others, as well as the impact others' styles have on them. The protocol closes with reflections on what individuals have learned about the different styles, or "directions," represented within the class, as well as how these differences may affect how students work together.

The protocol is very flexible; it can work with groups as small as 10 or as large as 60 or more. It often serves as an excellent team-building activity—usually provoking a good deal of laughter as groups gently poke fun at themselves and others. It can have long-term effects as well; for example, students commonly refer to their own and others' "directions" months later. North, South, East, and West become important descriptors for a range of genuine needs students may have for their participation in activities and discussions.

Compass Points can provide students and teachers with insight into both what individual students can contribute and what challenges, or even paralyzes, them in their interactions with others. For many students, making these conditions explicit can be a game changer in their ability to actively and productively participate in the classroom.

PURPOSES AND PREPARATION

Purposes
- To understand individual preferences for group work
- To understand how preferences may impact others

Habits Cultivated
- Understanding others' ideas and perspectives
- Understanding individual differences
- Self-reflection

Time
- Typically, 35–45 minutes, depending on the number of groups and the length of the follow-up discussion

Preparation
- **Set up the space.** Before the protocol begins, set up the room with prominent signs on the walls—North, South, East, and West. Make sure each station has sufficient space for a group of students to sit or stand. Have chart paper posted and markers available at each station.
- **Define the terms.** Create a handout with descriptions of the typical attributes of North, South, East, and West (see Step 1).

STEPS OF THE PROTOCOL

This version of the protocol is adapted from the School Reform Initiative website (see Resources). Times provided are guidelines and can be modified.

1. Introduction (5 minutes)
- Facilitator reviews the steps of the protocol, then distributes the handout describing the Compass Point directions and reviews it with the students.

    North: Acting—Likes to act, try things, plunge in. ("Let's do it!")

    South: Caring and communicating—Likes to know that everyone's thoughts and feelings have been taken into consideration, that their voices have been heard, and that

they understand what's expected before acting. ("Hold on,
let's hear from . . .")

East: Speculating—Likes to look at the big picture and explore
the possibilities before acting. ("Why are we doing this?
Have we considered . . . ?")

West: Paying attention to detail—Likes to know the who, what,
when, where, and why before acting. ("Okay, who's going
to go first? Where will we . . . ?")

The facilitator explains that while no one is really "only one
direction," most people tend to prefer one style over the others.

2. Selecting Individual Directions (1 minute)
- Facilitator asks students to select the *one* direction with which
they most identify. ("No Northeast allowed!")
- Students go to the space that has been set up for them near the
posted sign for their direction.

3. Small-Group Discussion (10–12 minutes)
- Each group is given the same prompts to respond to:
  » What are the strengths of our style (direction)?
  » What are the limitations or weaknesses of our style?
  » What other style do we find most difficult to work with and
  why?
  » What do the other direction groups need to know about us
  in order to work well together?
  » What do we value in each of the other styles?
- Groups discuss these prompts (*without* making notes on the
chart paper or newsprint) for 7–10 minutes. (Time can be
adjusted according to the size and the needs of the group.)
- Groups then jot key words for each question on chart paper.

4. Report Out (10–12 minutes)
- Each group, in turn, posts their chart paper and reports out.
- There is no discussion until after all the groups have reported out.

5. Debrief (10–12 minutes)
- Facilitator leads a discussion. Prompts for discussion may
include:
  » What did you learn?
  » What surprised you?

> » What do you notice about the distribution of people among
>   the directions? What do you think it might mean?
> » Why do other directions sometimes drive us crazy?
> » What did you learn from this experience that can help us
>   work together as a class and in small groups?

TIPS FOR FACILITATING THE PROTOCOL

- *Enjoy it!* Have fun with this activity. Each direction group (North,
  East, etc.) will almost always laugh at itself as it identifies its
  weaknesses and realizes how it can sometimes appear to others.
  Often one direction group's self-perceived strength is what
  another direction group identifies as the reason they can be
  difficult to work with. There is no right answer or best direction.
  The questions are designed to surface possible tensions and
  conflicts among different directions when they interact.
- *Keep the focus on the direction, not the person.* Encourage
  students to associate their observations and comments with
  a direction, rather than with individual people in the class
  (including themselves). This helps make the activity safe for
  everyone without stifling genuine concerns and conflicts.
- *Different-sized groups are fine.* Some groups will be larger;
  others, smaller. If you get a direction group of more than 12,
  divide students into two smaller groups for that direction so
  everyone gets a chance to talk. If only one or two students choose
  a particular direction, you might want to check in with them more
  frequently during the small-group portion of the protocol. During
  the debrief, be sure to invite students to think about what the
  varying group sizes might mean.
- *Be alert for labeling.* During debriefing, a student may draw
  the conclusion that all small groups should include at least one
  representative from each of the four directions. If this point
  surfaces, help students understand that, while the characteristics
  of all the directions contribute to productive group work, that
  doesn't translate into "one representative from each direction."
  Point out that each person possesses traits from all four directions
  and, therefore, can choose to take on the perspective of any of
  the compass points while engaged in small-group work. The goal

is not to label individuals but to make sure the qualities of each direction are represented in discussions and activities as needed. Once students understand this important point, they are likely to be more comfortable identifying themselves with more than one direction and have confidence that the qualities of each direction can be represented in group work, even if the small group does not include members drawn from each of the four direction groups that formed during the protocol.

COMPASS POINTS IN THE CLASSROOM

Daniel Velez is a special education teacher at Brooklyn College Academy, a public early college high school located in Brooklyn, New York. Daniel used Compass Points with his special education resource room class of 11 students. The protocol offered a tool to allow his students to examine their "strengths, weaknesses, and identification as students with special needs." His goal in using Compass Points initially was to support students' self-reflection, as well as to assess how the students identified themselves and how they were able to reveal themselves to their peers.

> I hoped to expose the students to opportunities for other types of leadership. For example, for a student who appropriately identified as a North, it was my goal to expose them to the other directions.

Daniel reviewed each of the direction descriptions with students, meeting with some individually, before they began the protocol.

When students identified their directions, the results surprised Daniel. There were five Norths, three Wests, two Souths, and one East.

> The Norths were made up of all males. While the other directions were chosen by females. Only one male confidently picked South. To my surprise, one of the Norths, however, originally identified as a South but broke away when he realized that his friends chose the more "dominant" traits.

Daniel's use of the protocol emphasized how valuable it can be in "allowing students to realize their unique leadership traits so that they can reach their true potential as leaders." It also revealed just how important others' perceptions are to students. Daniel saw how much "fitting in" mattered to the young man who switched from South to North once he saw where the other males in the class headed. "I wonder if he would have changed his mind if the other males were scattered among the directions."

Daniel's use of Compass Points led him to believe it would be an effective protocol to use at the beginning of the year and again at its end. Doing so would prompt students to reflect on their self-perception, as well as how it evolves, and could foster discussions about peer pressure and stereotyping. The following September, he decided to begin the year with Compass Points for all his classes—a mix of mainstream and special education students. Based on his earlier experience, he modified the prompts for the small-group discussions (Step 3) to: (1) Why is your direction more effective? (2) Which other direction do you want to work with and why? and (3) Which direction would you avoid working with? This time around, he noticed there were more Souths. He also noted that while there were only three Wests, students in all the other directions selected West as the direction with which they preferred to work. Students shared that this activity helped them to think about leadership in a new way, recognizing different types of leaders and not seeing "only Norths as leaders."

There are many ways to use Compass Points in the classroom. Carole Colburn, a middle school teacher (whose work is also described in Chapter 14: Tuning Protocol), uses it to support students in forming teams for class projects. She comments:

> Too often kids simply choose to be on teams based on whom they are friends with. Going through this protocol really helped them to think about the choice they were about to make. In the debriefing session, students shared that they wished they had known about these dominant styles in their past—thinking about past group projects that had not gone so well for them—and that they thought this information would really help them in the future working with teams and groups for class projects.

CHAPTER 5

Fears and Hopes

"Accentuate the positive, eliminate the negative"—so goes the familiar song. While no one would disagree that classrooms should be positive learning environments for all students, by recognizing those things that cause them concern or anxiety (the "negatives"), students can actually work together more positively and productively. When students are encouraged in a safe environment to say out loud what they fear about an upcoming class, test, or other school experience, they often become more open to taking a risk. In addition, when students share their fears and hopes with one another, they begin to build deeper bonds of trust that are essential to collaborative learning.

The Fears and Hopes protocol begins with asking students to reflect on both what they fear about an impending experience and what they hope for it. By design, students share their fears first and then their hopes. In discussing the group's fears and hopes, students may notice that fears and hopes are not as far apart as they might have initially thought. One person's fear may be another's hope, or an expressed fear may be alleviated by a hope that points toward a positive outcome. Sometimes students notice that the fears are the opposite outcome of the hopes, and that by expressing both, the class can brainstorm ways to allay fears and realize hopes.

Like Compass Points (Chapter 4), the Fears and Hopes protocol seeks to build the classroom community. Groups often use it at the outset of their work, sometimes as a way to set the stage for developing group norms. The protocol can be used at any transition point, for example, the beginning of a new unit or after a long break. While frequently used with a whole class, students can also use it when they form small groups. The protocol can help surface tensions around working together and deepen students' understanding of the goals for their shared task.

PURPOSES AND PREPARATION

Purposes
- To learn about each other
- To develop norms of group ownership and responsibility
- To bring concerns into the open and begin addressing them collectively

Habits Cultivated
- Articulating one's ideas and perspective
- Understanding others' ideas and perspectives
- Surfacing differences and uncomfortable feelings

Time
- Typically, 10–30 minutes, depending on the size of the group and the topic

Preparation
- **Materials.** The only supplies needed are writing materials for individual students (paper, index cards, etc.) and a whiteboard or chart paper to record the fears and the hopes students share out.

STEPS OF THE PROTOCOL

This version of the protocol is adapted from the School Reform Initiative website (see Resources). Times provided are guidelines and can be modified.

1. Introduction (2–4 minutes)
- Facilitator reviews the purposes and steps, reminding students of particular norms or guidelines to keep in mind as they work.

2. Reflecting on Fears and Hopes (3–5 minutes)
- Facilitator asks students to write down their greatest *fear* for the upcoming class or activity. Possible prompt: "If this were the worst class/activity you ever took part in, what might happen or not happen?"
- Facilitator asks students to write down their greatest *hope* for the upcoming class or activity. Possible prompt: "If this were the best

class/activity you ever took part in, what might happen or not happen? What would you learn?"

3. [Optional] Pair–Share (2 minutes)
- Facilitator asks students to share their hopes and fears with a partner.

4. Sharing out Fears and Hopes (3–10 minutes)
- Students share out *fears only* as the facilitator (or a recorder) lists them on the whiteboard or chart paper.
- Facilitator asks: What do you notice about our fears? Students respond verbally.
- Students share out *hopes only* as the facilitator (or a recorder) lists them on the whiteboard or chart paper.
- Facilitator asks: What do you notice about our hopes? Students respond verbally.

5. Debrief (5–10 minutes)
- Students reflect on their experiences in the protocol. Some prompts the facilitator might use include:
  - » What was surprising or interesting for you in doing this activity?
  - » How did sharing fears and hopes impact you or the group?
  - » How are you thinking now about the upcoming class or activity?

TIPS FOR FACILITATING THE PROTOCOL

- *Take on the role of facilitator yourself at first.* Because students may bring up sensitive topics in the discussion, we recommend the teacher facilitate the protocol—at least until students are familiar with it and know each other well.
- *Share your own fears and hopes.* You can help students to feel more comfortable by sharing some of your own fears and hopes, either before the protocol or by participating in the protocol itself.
- *Be true to students' wording.* The facilitator should list all fears and hopes as expressed, without edits, comments, or judgments.
- *Fears can be friends.* Remind students before and during the protocol that expressing their fears about an upcoming class or activity can help it go well for them and for the entire group.

FEARS AND HOPES IN THE CLASSROOM

Headwaters is a pre-K–12 independent school in Austin, Texas. Caitlin McDermott teaches science for Grades 9–12; Jaclyn Mann teaches English for Grades 6–8. Caitlin experienced Fears and Hopes in a workshop for new teachers at the school. She decided to try it on the first day of school with 9th- and 10th-grade students in her advisory group. (At Headwaters, advisory groups meet four times a week both to explore social and emotional topics and to provide students with academic support.) Because several of her advisory students were new to the school or returning after time away, and because Caitlin herself was new to the school, she thought Fears and Hopes would be a good way to build community.

Caitlin modified the protocol to work with the special first-day schedule, which called for advisory groups to meet once in the morning and again in the afternoon. In the morning meeting, Caitlin handed students index cards and gave them 6–7 minutes to write their fears for the new school year on one side of the card and hopes on the other. She asked students not to write names on the cards, anticipating that anonymity would make them more willing to share their true fears and hopes. After students had finished writing, she gave them the option to share out, mindful that some might not be comfortable sharing their feelings in the new school environment. Finally, Caitlin asked students to turn in their cards.

During her lunch break, Caitlin compiled the fears and hopes as the students had written them and typed them in a randomized way on a shared document. She explained, "I didn't want there to be giveaways as to who was who—I wanted students to maintain anonymity." When the students came back for the afternoon session, she projected the document and asked students what they noticed about the fears and the hopes. There were moments of humor, with some students poking fun at themselves for their comments. For example, one said, "I am hopeful that I will like other people more than I usually do." During the discussion, the student who wrote it volunteered, good-naturedly, "I mean, I like all of you, but in general I just don't like that many people." Other students chuckled.

Caitlin felt that doing the protocol gave new students comfort since they could see and discuss the ways their concerns were like those of returning students. The students concluded that they shared with classmates many of the same fears and hopes, and that the fears were often the reverse of the hopes. One student reflected, "I know I want to get good grades, and that is a goal, but I also fear failing—even though I know it's unlikely I will fail given my usual grades. They are opposite of each other."

As part of debriefing the protocol, Caitlin asked the students to rate it using the "fist-to-five technique" (showing a fist equals the lowest rating, five fingers indicates the highest); most gave it four out of five. She reflected:

> Next time I would wait a week into the school year because of the class dynamic. There were a whole lot of jitters. After a couple of weeks together I began to see people coming out of their shell, and I would be curious if their answers would differ in doing Fears and Hopes at this point. I also plan to try Fears and Hopes in my Biology class before our first big assessment.

Jaclyn Mann used Fears and Hopes in her English class with incoming 6th graders. Unlike Caitlin, she did ask students to write their names on their index cards before collecting them. A few weeks into the school year, she reviewed the cards and found that some of their concerns were playing out—for example, those who feared being late to class had been late. Knowing the students' fears helped Jaclyn to adjust how she interpreted and redirected certain student behaviors. She planned to give the cards back to the students at the end of the semester, as a way for the students to reflect on their growth. Jaclyn also thought that using Fears and Hopes would be a good way to introduce an upcoming unit on poetry—a topic that often brings up a range of feelings for many students.

As these teachers' stories demonstrate, Fears and Hopes provides a tool for students and teachers to understand what may hold them back from doing their best work together—and, ultimately, help everyone to achieve success.

CHAPTER 6

Microlab

The Microlab protocol offers an opportunity for all of the individuals in a group both to share their perspective and to listen carefully to the perspectives of others. This protocol is designed to allow a group to talk about an important question (usually one framed by the teacher). Sitting or standing in groups of three, each student in the group has a designated amount of time (typically, just 1 to 2 minutes) to respond to the question while the other two students simply listen.

While the design of this protocol is simple, using it fosters thought-ful discussion and cultivates listening and perspective-taking skills. Unlike most protocols, this one does not usually include a facilitator within the group; rather the teacher or another facilitator provides directions and calls time (strictly!) for all the small groups, which work in parallel. The Microlab provides a clear and inclusive structure for students to discuss their ideas about curriculum topics, reflect on questions about their own learning, or share perspectives on the cul-ture of the classroom, the school, or the society they live in.

The Microlab is based on the Constructivist Listening Protocol developed by Julian Weissglass (1990) from the National Coalition for Equity at the University of California, Santa Barbara. The version shared here includes a brief period of quiet following each person's sharing, further encouraging thoughtful reflection on alternative perspectives.

PURPOSES AND PREPARATION

Purposes
- To address a question so that each member of the group gets a chance to respond
- To listen to others' perspectives on the question

Habits Cultivated
- Reflecting on a question
- Articulating one's ideas and perspective
- Listening attentively

Time
- Typically, 15–20 minutes. This estimate is for a single round of everyone responding to one question. However, additional rounds (usually based on additional questions that build on the original question) and/or an optional open discussion period following the round(s) require additional time.

Preparation
- *Frame a compelling question.* The most important thing is to develop a compelling question that matters to the group. Usually, a more complex and open-ended question—one about which students are likely to hold differing perspectives—works best. (If you decide to do the protocol with multiple rounds, choose questions that build upon one another.)
- *Set up the space to encourage listening.* Invite students to pull their desks or chairs close together. (Sitting close to their groupmates helps students hear—the room can get loud when a third of them are talking at once.) Some teachers ask students to stand in tight clusters. Asking students to stand makes it easier for students to create groups with classmates they don't usually sit next to. Standing has the added advantage of giving students the opportunity to move around—an important consideration, given how much of the day students (especially older ones) typically spend sitting.
- *Remind students about confidentiality.* Make sure, in student-friendly language, that everyone understands what confidentiality means (e.g., "When somebody trusts us enough to tell us something personal, we make sure not to share that thing with other people.").

STEPS OF THE PROTOCOL

This version of the Microlab is adapted from *The Facilitator's Book of Questions: Tools for Looking Together at Student and Teacher Work*, 3rd edition (see Resources). Times provided are guidelines only and can be modified.

1. Introduction (3–5 minutes)
Facilitator reviews the protocol's steps and guidelines, allowing time for students to ask clarifying questions. Guidelines include:

• Each student gets equal time to speak. To ensure this equity, talk must stop when time is called.
• If the speaker finishes before time is called, the group maintains silence, using the time for additional reflection.
• Listeners do not interrupt, interpret, paraphrase, analyze, give advice, or ask questions while the speaker is talking.
• Confidentiality should be maintained.
• The speaker should not criticize or complain about the listeners or others during her turn.

2. Forming Triads (1 minute)
• Facilitator invites students to form triads, numbering off within each—1, 2, 3. Some teachers prefer to have students "count off" to form the trios. (They should count off by the number of total groups of three you will have in the end: 30 students in a class means having students count to 10. For groups that don't divide by three, see "Do the Math" in Tips for Facilitating the Protocol.)

3. Reflecting on the Question (1–3 minutes)
• Facilitator shares the question, reading it twice. Students have a brief period of silence, usually 30 seconds to 2 minutes, to reflect on it. (They may want to write or sketch as they reflect silently.)

4. Responding and Listening in Rounds (5–7 minutes)
• At the end of the initial period of reflection, facilitator invites those who are number 1's in the triads to begin speaking,

reminding them of the time limit (usually 1–2 minutes, depending on the complexity of the question). Facilitator also reminds number 2's and 3's in each group that they are to listen without interrupting the speaker in any way.

- Facilitator then invites everyone to begin the period of silent reflection (which could be anywhere from 15 seconds to 1 minute or longer, though the duration should be announced to the group and kept consistent throughout the protocol).
- Facilitator then invites the number 2's in each group to begin (while 1's and 3's listen silently).
- The process continues, with periods of speaking alternating with periods of silence until all three group members have had the chance to speak.
- A final period of silent reflection follows the last speaker.

5. [Optional] Additional Rounds for Additional Questions (5–7 minutes per round)

- If the group is addressing more than one question, the same process of alternating periods of speaking with periods of silence is used for the additional question(s).
- Rotate order: Typically, in the second round (addressing a second question), the 2's speak first (followed by the 3's, then the 1's). In the third round (addressing a third question), the 3's speak first, followed by the 1's, then the 2's.

6. [Optional] Open Discussion in Triads and/or Large Group (5 minutes)

- Facilitator may opt to conclude the structured rounds with a brief period (usually 5–10 minutes) of open discussion in triads and/or in the large group. The discussion might be framed in several ways, depending on the emphasis, for example:
  » What did you learn about the question that the group answered—either through your own reflection or through listening to others?
  » Were there puzzles for you in the comments that other people shared?
  » What new questions do you have now about this topic?

7. Debrief (5 minutes)
- Students reflect on their experience of the protocol. Facilitator might ask:
  - » What was it like to use this protocol?
  - » How is it different from typical conversation?
  - » What was helpful about this protocol? What was difficult?
  - » Based on your experience of speaking, listening, and responding in this protocol, which of these skills do you think you most need to work on?

TIPS FOR FACILITATING THE PROTOCOL

- ***Experiment with the timing.*** For younger students (or even older ones using the protocol for the first time), try using shorter times (perhaps half a minute to 1 minute) for both responding as well as reflecting silently. You can also adjust the times to suit the question you are asking students to respond to, allowing more time for more complex questions (though generally not longer than 2 minutes).
- ***Emphasize listening.*** Before you do this protocol for the first time, have a short discussion with students about listening: When do they do their best listening? What does that feel like? What keeps them from listening well? What strategies might they use to help them listen better? Encourage them to use these listening strategies during the protocol. In between the rounds of the protocol, you might offer additional reminders to students to draw on these strategies.
- ***Acknowledge that sitting quietly can be uncomfortable.*** The periods of silent reflection may be difficult for some students. You might try keeping these periods relatively short at first (15–20 seconds) and work up to longer periods of time as you repeat the protocol over the course of weeks or months.
- ***Do the math.*** If the whole group does not divide evenly by three, you might have one or more groups of four students. The process should still be the same for everybody in the room (that is, equal amount of time to speak), but the groups of three have time for open discussion while person 4 in the groups of four is talking.

MICROLAB IN THE CLASSROOM

Charlie Shryock, an Advanced Placement (AP) literature teacher (and currently academic dean) at Bishop McNamara High School (BMHS) in Forestville, Maryland, contemplated several ways to support his students in developing cultural competency, an important school-wide goal. He chose the Microlab as the right tool for opening the often-sensitive discussion about identity and inclusion. In the past, he had opted for an open-ended conversation, but, as Charlie pointed out:

> One feature of free-flowing conversation is that we tend
> to see uneven participation from students, based upon all
> sorts of factors—for example, their interest in the topic, their
> willingness to take risks in sharing newly formed ideas, and their
> assumptions about how others will listen to them.

He hoped that the Microlab, with its timed rounds and its focus on listening, "might provide space for more hesitant speakers to share their thoughts and, at the same time, challenge the more active speakers to listen with intent. In other words, everyone would be challenged a little to 'show up' in the conversation in a new way."

Charlie was also eager for his students to have the experience of allowing ideas to linger before rushing on to the next one: "Too frequently, participants in a free-flowing conversation will 'step on' silence, which means that some ideas don't have time to 'breathe.'" Charlie felt that the guidelines for timed rounds in the Microlab would ensure that the entire group would have "blank space" for reflection. Given the importance and the complexity of the issues of identity and inclusion, it seemed especially important to him that students have the time to sit with one another's thoughts before responding.

Charlie chose to do the full three rounds of the Microlab. In each round, Charlie posed a question, to which the students, seated in triads, took turns responding.

1. How comfortable are you talking about race and culture here at BMHS?
2. Which identities are invisible or hard to see here at BMHS?
3. If these identities were more visible, easier to see, what would that look like? If we were more inclusive, what would we see?

At the end of the third round, following the final period of quiet reflection, the students took part in a few minutes of open discussion in their group.

Both Charlie and the students shared positive reflections on the experience. "Students rarely have a situation in which they're really being listened to," Charlie commented. "And they are starved for communication. They need to connect with each other. That's what their technology focus is all about. This is a way for them to connect without the phone screen."

The students described the conversation as "refreshing" and "thought-provoking." "The part where we had to be quiet was really hard," one student commented. Others noted how the silence made them more aware of their own thoughts and how they react to people. "We're not used to being listened to for so long," commented another student. "That felt good."

For Charlie and his students, the Microlab gave them a way to begin an important and ongoing conversation. "Did we come up with complete answers to all of those questions? No, of course not," Charlie said. "We needed a place to start, and the Microlab let us get some important ideas out that we could come back to later."

CHAPTER 7

Chalk Talk

The Chalk Talk protocol's name hearkens to a time when chalk and blackboards, along with overhead projectors and pull-down maps, dominated the classroom. While these may seem like quaint artifacts, as teachers move to white boards, Smart Boards, tablets, and other presentation and communication technologies, the purposes for the protocol and the habits it cultivates are more relevant than ever.

Chalk Talk was developed by Hilton Smith of the Foxfire Fund and adapted by Marilyn Wentworth of the National School Reform Faculty, then based at the Coalition of Essential Schools. It supports groups in a *silent* conversation, during which participants can work on problems, share ideas, and reflect on one another's thinking. The conversation is carried out through the students' writing—on a blackboard, white board, or sheets of chart paper taped to the walls or laid flat on tables.

Chalk Talk is an extremely flexible protocol, allowing students and teachers to discuss almost any question or topic. The discussion may take just a few minutes or most of the class period. It is especially powerful for students who may struggle to express themselves orally, as it gives them time to think about and craft their responses—not always easy in a rapid-fire discussion. It also works well paired with other protocols, as in the classroom example that follows, which combines Chalk Talk with the Gallery Walk protocol (see Chapter 12).

PURPOSES AND PREPARATION

Purposes
- To reflect on a question or topic
- To generate ideas or solve problems
- To make thinking visible

Habits Cultivated
- Articulating one's ideas and perspective
- Making connections to others' ideas and perspectives
- Clarifying thoughts, ideas, questions, concepts, etc.

Time
- Chalk Talk can be completed in as little as 5 minutes; however, to allow all students ample time to think and write, 15–20 minutes is a good estimate.

Preparation
- ***Prepare space and materials.*** Whether using a whiteboard, chart paper taped to the wall, or other materials, the Chalk Talk requires plenty of space for students to write and draw. Students should also have easy access to writing implements appropriate for the surface. (Students often appreciate a choice of colors.)
- ***Identify the focusing question or topic.*** The Chalk Talk protocol is typically initiated by the framing of a question or a topic that relates to what students are reading, discussing, or studying. The question or topic is meant to stimulate students' reflection on their own learning. The teacher (and students) may develop the question or topic in advance or they may use the Chalk Talk protocol on the spur of the moment to explore a question, an idea, or a problem that has emerged in their discussion, research, etc. Good questions and topics are open-ended and provoke a range of student ideas and perspectives.

STEPS OF THE PROTOCOL

The version of Chalk Talk below is adapted from the School Reform Initiative website (see Resources). Times provided are guidelines and can be modified.

1. Introduction (2–3 minutes)
- Facilitator reviews the purposes and the steps of the protocol.
- Facilitator reviews specific guidelines, including:
  - » Chalk Talk is a *silent* activity; no one may talk at all.

» Students may add their own ideas to the Chalk Talk with words or graphics as they please.

» Students can also comment on other people's ideas using words or graphics (for example, drawing a line to connect related comments, circling or placing stars next to ideas they like or agree with, etc.).

2. Naming the Question or Topic (1 minute)

• Facilitator writes a relevant question or topic for reflection—in a circle, in big letters—on the board or on a piece of chart paper.

3. Chalk-Talking (5–10 minutes)

• Using chalk, markers, or other appropriate tools, students write on the surfaces, writing when they like and in the manner they choose. For example, students may write comments, ask questions, draw images or other graphics, or use lines or arrows to make connections among comments.

4. Calling Time (1 minute)

• Facilitator lets the group know that writing time is over, either when the designated time is up or when students' contributions seem to be tapering off.

5. Open Discussion (3–5 minutes)

• Facilitator asks students to respond *orally* to what has emerged in the silent discussion. Possible questions include:

» What do you notice about what we wrote?

» What new ideas came up for you?

» What do you wonder about now?

6. Debrief (5 minutes)

• Facilitator asks students to reflect on their experiences of the Chalk Talk protocol, for example:

» How did Chalk Talk support your thinking about the question or the topic?

» How does "Chalk Talking" relate to other discussions we have in class?

» How could the Chalk Talk protocol be changed to support our thinking more effectively?

TIPS FOR FACILITATING THE PROTOCOL

- *Intervene with caution.* As a facilitator, you may choose simply to observe how the silent discussion unfolds for your students. You might also decide to engage in the discussion yourself, for example, by circling an interesting idea, making a connection between two or more ideas, sharing your own written comment, or commenting on a student's comment by writing next to it. Doing any of these will have an impact on the discussion— perhaps refocusing it around the original question or topic or sending it in a new direction. Be aware that students are likely to see your contributions as having more authority than theirs, and this perception may inhibit emerging student-to-student dialogue. Avoid commenting out loud during the Chalk Talk!

- *Call time judiciously.* The heart of Chalk Talk is when students are communicating about the question or idea through their writing, drawing, circling, etc. The facilitator decides when to call time for this step. Sometimes it needs to end simply because there is no more time in the class period. If this is the case, try to give students a 1- to 2-minute warning so they can finish their thoughts. If not pressed for time, allow for "wait time" during a lull between comments. This pause may give students the time they need to process what others have written before they continue to add further comments or questions.

CHALK TALK IN THE CLASSROOM

Christopher Barley uses Chalk Talk, which he calls "Chart Talk," with his Spanish 1 and 2 students at Essex Street Academy, a small public high school on the Lower East Side of New York City. For Chris, the protocol is a powerful tool for reviewing content and preparing students for tests and other assessments, as well as enabling students to generate their own questions for assessments—thus creating more student ownership of the curriculum. Chris often combines the Chalk Talk protocol with a brief Gallery Walk (see Chapter 12 for full protocol) to support students in reviewing content from the unit. Together, both protocols take a full 50-minute class period.

Chris' use of Chalk Talk incorporates individual, small-group, and whole-group work. To allow for the movement necessary in the protocol, he sets up the desks in clusters and makes sure classroom walls are free to post sheets of chart paper. He serves as facilitator and timekeeper for the protocol.

Students begin by reviewing their notes and other materials related to the unit topic, for example, "the family," "house and home," and so on. Individually, students write a reflection in Spanish on a piece of paper on their clipboard. Then Chris arranges students into groups of four or five. Each group has a single piece of chart paper with the topic written on it, for example, *La Comida* (Food). For the next 5–7 minutes, students use markers to silently share their ideas on the topic. Chris tells students: "Write or draw anything that comes to mind when you think of food." Their writing here is predominantly in Spanish.

Each group then posts its chart paper on the wall for a brief gallery walk. For about 5–7 minutes, the groups circulate, looking at other groups' charts. As they do, students make notes on their clipboards, adding to their own knowledge about the topic, as well as noticing patterns, surprises, or interesting items from other groups. Chris encourages students to add images, make connections, and write on other groups' charts during the gallery walk. He tells them, "*¡Más ideas!* Keep the generative spirit going!"

After students have had a chance to visit each of the other groups' charts, the small groups discuss what they found interesting or what their group might have missed. Then in the whole-class group, Chris facilitates a discussion about the patterns students noticed, what they did not see that might be important to the topic, and any remaining questions. Here, too, the discussion is mostly in Spanish; however, Chris adds, "in the case of reviewing material, it may be helpful for students to ask clarifying questions in English to make sure there are no lingering doubts about meaning, usage, etc."

Finally, on an index card, each group creates a section of the quiz based on what they have seen and heard. Some examples include: "¿Cuáles comidas no son frutas?" ("Which foods are not fruits?") and "Fill in the blank: '*Mi verdura favorita es* _____.'" ("My favorite vegetable is _____.") Groups have also created matching activities, prompts to draw a picture, and clues for crossword puzzles. Chris collects the ideas and uses them in creating the unit assessment.

In reflecting on his use of Chalk Talk with students, Chris says, "It helps students organize their thinking around a subject or topic." He points out the value of proceeding from individual to small group, and finally, to large group in the gallery walk:

It's important for students to do that individual brainstorming first so that they come to understand through the process where their blind spots are, where their gaps in knowledge are. Later, they'll go around and look at the charts and fill in some of those. It's about understanding what you know and what you need to know.

Students also appreciate the collaborative approach to review. Chris comments: "It's a student-produced review, where they are coming up with what's important for the assessment. And they like to move." He contrasts Chalk Talk with more typical approaches to learning language: "In terms of language classes, often students get a list of vocabulary: 'Know these words. . . .' A lot of students get stuck on that: How do you know what's important? What to study?" Chalk Talk helps students make the gaps in their language visible and provides an engaging way to address them.

CHAPTER 8

Peeling the Onion

The educators who developed Peeling the Onion describe it as a "defining the problem" protocol. They recognized that often, when faced with a challenge, people tend to make decisions or take actions without understanding what makes it a challenge to begin with. The Peeling the Onion protocol focuses on understanding the layers or multiple dimensions of the problem rather than solving it. Having used the protocol to develop a better understanding, the student presenter (the "keeper of the problem") who shares her problem with the group is then in a stronger position to take next steps, which might involve solving the problem, managing it in a different way, or sometimes even setting it aside (at least temporarily).

At the heart of Peeling the Onion is a series of rounds, each one prompting the group to engage with the presenter's dilemma or problem in different ways, for example, reflecting on what they heard the presenter describe, identifying possible assumptions, raising questions, etc. As in some other protocols, the presenter listens silently during these rounds, as others discuss her problem.

While the focus is typically on one student's problem or dilemma, other students in the group learn from the process of peeling the onion together. They might be able to apply ideas that emerge in the protocol to a similar problem they themselves have encountered. More importantly, the protocol helps them develop the habit of resisting the impulse to leap to solutions until they have a better understanding of the dimensions of the problem.

PURPOSES AND PREPARATION

Purpose
- To explore a problem or dilemma

Habits Cultivated
- Articulating one's ideas and perspective
- Understanding others' ideas and perspectives
- Resisting the inclination to solve a problem before understanding it

Time
- Approximately 35–45 minutes; time will vary according to the size of the group(s).

Preparation
- ***Preconference with presenter, as needed.*** Depending on the presenter's familiarity with the protocol, the facilitator usually checks in briefly with her about the problem or dilemma she would like to present. The facilitator and the presenter should make sure the problem or dilemma is a genuine one for the presenter—one she doesn't know how to solve on her own and about which she is eager to get feedback from others.
- ***Help the presenter develop a focusing question.*** The presenter frames a question (or statement) about the problem or dilemma so that the group can provide focused feedback. The facilitator might also suggest that she jot down a few notes to prepare for her presentation.

STEPS OF THE PROTOCOL

This version of the protocol is adapted from the Peeling the Onion: Defining a Problem protocol on the School Reform Initiative website (see Resources). Times are approximate and can be modified.

1. Introduction (2–4 minutes)
- Facilitator reviews purpose and steps of the protocol, reminding students of any norms or guidelines that the group has decided on or that seem especially important for the protocol.

2. Describing the Problem/Dilemma (3–5 minutes)
- Presenter (also known as the keeper of the problem) describes the problem/dilemma.
- Presenter asks a focusing question.

3. Clarifying Questions (3 minutes)

- Students ask strictly informational questions. Presenter responds to each briefly.

4. Rounds (15–20 minutes)

- In each discussion round, students speak to the same prompt (see below). Group does not move on to the next round until each participant has had an opportunity to respond to the guiding prompt. (Note: Facilitator may choose to repeat a round if additional responses seem to be emerging.)
- *Prompts for rounds (in order):*
  » What I heard [the presenter] say is . . .
  » One assumption that seems to be part of the dilemma is . . . or One thing I assume to be true about this problem is . . .
  » A question this raises for me is . . .
  » Other questions this raises for me are . . .
  » What if . . . ? or Have we thought about . . . ? or I wonder . . .
- During each round, presenter listens *silently* and may take notes.

5. Presenter's Reflection (3 minutes)

- Presenter reviews notes and reflects aloud on what she is learning.
- Participants listen *silently* and may take notes.

6. Now What? (5 minutes)

- Presenter and participants talk about the possibilities and options that have surfaced in relation to the dilemma or problem. (Note: Facilitator should remind students that this step is not meant to resolve the dilemma or solve the problem.)

7. Debrief (5 minutes)

- Questions to guide reflection may include:
  » How was this like peeling an actual onion?
  » What about the protocol was useful? Challenging?
  » How might we use this protocol in the future?

TIPS FOR FACILITATING THE PROTOCOL

- *Clarify "clarifying."* Although Step 3 calls for clarifying questions, students are often tempted to ask probing questions or even offer solutions to the dilemma. Remind them that clarifying questions ask for information only. The presenter should be able to answer them very briefly.
- *Define "reflecting back."* In the first round of Step 4 (responding to "What I heard the presenter say is . . ."), it can be challenging for students to avoid making assumptions about or interpretations of the problem/dilemma. Remind them that this step is only for reflecting back what they heard the presenter describe; in other words, collectively putting together a picture of the problem *as the presenter sees it.*
- *Post it.* Students who speak towards the end of the round may forget what they were originally going to say. Cynthia Elkins, one of the teachers in the story that follows, suggests providing students with sticky notes to write down their thoughts. "It's not just a memory strategy," she adds, "it's a reinforcement of the value of feedback."

PEELING THE ONION IN THE CLASSROOM

The Eagle Rock School in Estes Park, Colorado, is a year-round residential, full-scholarship high school made up of 72 students from across the country—students who did not experience success in traditional schools. The school does not use traditional grade levels. The staff regularly uses protocols for professional development, and many teachers use protocols in classes with students.

Co-teachers Cynthia Elkins, the art instructional specialist, and Josán Perales, the world languages instructional specialist, teach a course called "Recrearte," in which students aged 16–19 use books, articles, art, and field trips to answer the question: "Why consider sustainable practices?" Students work in groups to research a particular environmental concern and the ways in which sustainable practices can help to address that concern. The project culminates in a student-made art gallery and presentation at the local public library.

Cindy and Josán recognized that the student groups developed their research focus at different rates and decided to use Peeling the

Onion to support the group having the most difficulty honing in on a thesis. Cindy explained, "We felt the protocol fit perfectly. The students are looking at dilemmas daily, and we thought it would be great to take one of the tools we are taught in our professional development and share that with students." The co-teachers felt the protocol would help students to "take a hard look at their projects," to help them make some choices and "throw out fluff and dive in deep."

Cindy set the stage for Peeling the Onion by reminding students that using a protocol for the first time can feel frustrating, but "the more you use protocols, the more you see the beauty of what they're asking you to do." Since the protocol was new to students, Cindy and Josán co-facilitated so that the students could focus on participating in the process.

In the first step of the protocol, the presenting group explained that they felt their focus, deforestation, was too big, and that they were having trouble deciding how to narrow it. After some clarifying questions, Cindy and Josán guided the students through the rounds in Step 4. In the first round, students noted the presenters' experience of "feeling stuck." In the subsequent rounds, they identified some assumptions the presenters might have made, raised questions, and shared "I wonders . . ." to push the presenters' thinking.

After listening to the whole group respond to each of the prompts, the presenting group members reflected on what they had heard. They discussed the idea of focusing on "the ways palm kernel oil is being harvested in the rainforest in Indonesia and Malaysia, and the impact on orangutans, local culture, and the world." In the following step, Now What?, the full group brainstormed some actions the presenters might take to complete their research and create a presentation. Building on the ideas generated in the protocol, the presenting group went on to develop as a culminating project a "tree of life" sculpture made from discarded products containing palm kernel oil.

During the debrief, one student commented, "I like working with a team and getting new ideas." Another reflected that using the protocol "makes me feel professional, like I'm doing a real-life job." The presenters said they felt relieved and that the protocol had been useful in helping them to move forward on their project.

Overall, the teachers felt the protocol was a good fit for their students and for this purpose. Cindy commented: "Students had clear ideas of how to proceed at the end of the protocol." Josán added: "By having students both present their ideas and support their peers, they all could authentically take ownership over the problem-solving process, collectively act as a team, and feel confident in completing the project."

Josán noted some of the ideas that came up more easily in early rounds were explored more deeply in subsequent ones. At times, however, it was necessary for one of the teachers to step in when students tried to solve the problem rather than staying focused on understanding it. The teachers identified several modifications to the protocol that they planned to make in the future, including creating project-specific sentence stems for getting started in the rounds and establishing a note-taking system to record ideas as they came up—another way of emphasizing the power of a group's thinking about a problem.

CHAPTER 9

Text Rendering Experience

Text rendering is an approach to reading developed by Peter Elbow and teachers at the Bard Institute for Writing and Thinking. The deceptively simple exercise they created turns out to be a powerful tool for supporting readers *at all skill levels* to enter a text—the first stage in being able to make meaning of the text.

In the Text Rendering Experience, students share out sentences, phrases, and words that stand out to them *for any reason*—they liked the way it sounded, found it interesting, were confused by it, etc. The goal is not to identify the main point of the passage, but, as Elbow and Belanoff (2000, p. 7) have written, to notice "the sections or passages that seem to resonate or linger in mind or be sources of energy."

The Text Rendering Experience is flexible: It can be used with written texts of all types. It is often used to support students entering into a text for the first time. It can also be used as a strategy for going deeper with a text that has been read (at least) once before, as in Crystal Fresco Gifford's classroom, described in the following section. It can also be used with spoken or recorded texts, usually with students following along with written transcripts. The Text Rendering Experience is often followed by a discussion or writing activity in which students respond to, interpret, make connections to, or analyze the text in some way.

While the Text Rendering Experience can be used even with the most expert readers, it is an especially powerful tool in helping struggling readers, including language learners, to find their voices in responding to a text.

PURPOSES AND PREPARATION

Purposes
- To enter a text
- To collectively make meaning of a text

Habits Cultivated

- Reading closely
- Paying attention to detail and nuance

Time

- Typically, 15–25 minutes. Timing depends on the length and complexity of the text, size of groups, and length of the discussion that follows the three rounds of sharing out. In general, sharing out does not take very long, since there is no discussion in between speakers. However, having a "scribe" adds a few extra seconds between speakers. If the text being examined is spoken or recorded, it may be helpful to listen to it twice.

Preparation

- ***Choose the text carefully.*** Text rendering generally works best with a text that is short enough to be read by all participants within a relatively brief period, so that everyone is focused on the same portion of text—whether a paragraph or few pages. The protocol tends to work better with texts that are more narrative, imaginative, or poetic than purely informational (for example, a set of directions).
- ***Give the students the text and the tools they need.*** Make sure students have a clean and easily legible copy of the text to annotate by underlining the sentence, phrase, or word that stands out to them. If students cannot write on the text, give them sticky notes on which to write their sentences, phrases, and words, and ask them to attach the sticky notes to the relevant places in the text.
- ***To scribe or not to scribe?*** Consider having a "scribe" (recorder) for each small group, especially if the protocol is setting up an activity with the same text (for example, a discussion, writing assignment, etc.). The scribe records on chart paper or white board the sentences, phrases, and words that students share out exactly as students say them (no paraphrasing!).

STEPS OF THE PROTOCOL

The protocol below is adapted from the Text Rendering Experience from the School Reform Initiative website (see Resources). Note: In this protocol, some of the steps are presented as "rounds" because participants go in order around the circle. Times provided are guide-lines only and can be modified.

1. Introduction (1–2 minutes)
- Facilitator reviews the purposes and steps ("rounds") of the protocol and reminds participants that it is appropriate to repeat a sentence, phrase, or word that another participant has shared.

2. First Round: Sentences (2–3 minutes)
- Each student shares a *sentence* from the text that she thinks or feels is particularly significant. (The scribe records each sentence.)

3. Second Round: Phrases (2–3 minutes)
- Each student shares a *phrase* from the text that she thinks or feels is particularly significant. (The scribe records each phrase.)

4. Third Round: Words (2–3 minutes)
- Each student shares the *word* from the text that she thinks or feels is particularly significant. (The scribe records each word.)

5. Discussion (5–10 minutes)
- Students discuss what they have heard and what this may say about the text. Some possible prompts for the discussion:
  » What did you notice about the sentences, phrases, and words your classmates (and you) shared?
  » What might this say about the text?
  » What ideas or insights about the text does looking at it this way suggest?
  » What questions about the text does looking at it this way raise?

6. Debrief (3–5 minutes)
- Students reflect on their experience of the protocol. Some questions to start this discussion might include:
  » What was interesting or eye opening to you about the protocol?
  » If you heard someone repeat your sentence, phrase, or word, how did that feel?
  » What did it make you think about?
  » What might we change to make the protocol more effective or meaningful?

TIPS FOR FACILITATING THE PROTOCOL

- *Model it.* Model what you mean by underlining a sentence, a phrase, and a word. You can easily do this with another text that is not being read for the protocol or, in some cases, an earlier part the same text. Phrases may be a difficult concept for some students to grasp.
- *Take a beat.* In introducing the protocol or between rounds, suggest that students "take a beat" (a second or two) between the person who shared before them and their own sharing out. This builds in a little time for individuals and the group to process each student's contribution.
- *Pass it on.* While encouraging all students to participate in every round, let students know that they can pass if they did not come up with a contribution (sentence, phrase, word) for that particular round. Remind students that an important part of learning through text rendering comes from listening to others.

TEXT RENDERING EXPERIENCE IN THE CLASSROOM

Crystal Fresco Gifford, of Shorecrest High School, Shoreline, Washington, uses the Text Rendering Experience with her 7th- through 12th-grade history classes, which typically include English language learners (ELLs) as well as native English speakers.

Crystal combines the protocol with a focused reading activity in which students write down a focus question, either one she gives them or one they develop on their own. For example, when reading the first chapter of Joy Hakim's *A History of Us* (1997), students underline or highlight the text in relation to the question, "Why do we study history?" In pairs, students follow along as Crystal reads the text aloud, marking the text. Crystal often pairs English language learners with native English-speaking students. For each page or section of the text, students summarize in relation to their focus question.

This sets the stage for the Text Rendering Experience, in which the purpose shifts from reading with a specific focus to being able to, as Crystal puts it, "dialogue using evidence from the text." Students work in groups of four and five, with a student facilitator and a scribe in each group. Crystal acts as timekeeper for all groups. In most cases, students complete both the focused reading activity and the Text Rendering Experience within one 50-minute class.

In the next day's class, students sometimes create "found poems," using the shared-out sentences, phrases, and words (recorded by the scribes) from the previous day's Text Rendering Experience. As Crystal describes, this is a way for students to "publish the knowledge they have gained from reading, speaking, and listening." In other cases, students may complete an essay drawing on what they learned through the processes of focused reading and text rendering.

For Crystal, the power of the Text Rendering Experience, in combination with the other activities, is that it reinforces and integrates students' abilities to "use all four domains of learning—reading, writing, speaking, and listening." She finds it especially helpful for ELL students:

> The process of "deconstructing" the text for meaning with a focus has helped ELL students build confidence in both their reading of the English language and comprehension of the text. With practice, it empowers ELL students to self-select the word, phrase, and sentence that resonates with them the most. My ELL students are now given a voice they would not necessarily have had.

For Crystal and other teachers, the Text Rendering Experience provides a tool to support all students to engage with their classmates in accessing and making meaning of texts.

CHAPTER 10

Save the Last Word for Me

To have the last word in a discussion is usually associated with an abrupt and forceful end of a dispute, a kind of verbal door slamming. The Save the Last Word for Me protocol turns this idea on its head: It is structured to open discussion and deepen understanding among participants, allowing them collectively to make new meaning of the text. Developed by Patricia Averette, Save the Last Word for Me supports students in clarifying and understanding a text through speaking, listening, and building on one another's ideas. Like the Text Rendering Experience (Chapter 9), it can be used with texts from any subject area, grade level, and genre.

Save the Last Word for Me begins with students individually reading a common text and highlighting a passage that represents for them the most significant idea in the text. In groups, students then take turns being the presenter, sharing their selected passage with the group but not saying why they chose it. The other students in the group take turns commenting on the passage while the presenter listens but does not respond. The presenter gets the "last word," sharing her original reason for highlighting the passage, reflecting on other students' perspectives on it, and offering any new ideas about the passage that have emerged from listening to the group. This process is repeated until each member of the group has had a chance to be the presenter.

Save the Last Word for Me is a variation of The Final Word, a protocol developed by Patricia Averette and Daniel Baron. In The Final Word, the presenter shares her perspective *before* hearing from others—a small but important difference. Both protocols can be used as a tool for entering a new text or at any point in working with a text, and both lend themselves to many follow-up activities. For example, after completing the protocol, students can respond to the text in writing using ideas and textual evidence that emerged during discussion. Alternatively, the protocol can be used as a "preactivity" that leads into a large-group discussion.

PURPOSES AND PREPARATION

Purposes
- To enter a text
- To collectively make meaning of a text

Habits Cultivated
- Referencing textual evidence
- Understanding others' ideas and perspectives
- Synthesizing others' ideas

Time
- Typically 35–45 minutes, not including individual reading of the text. Each round lasts approximately 5–7 minutes; thus, a group of four should complete all four rounds in about 20–25 minutes. Note: Including an open dialogue about the text following the last round and before the debrief step adds time.

Preparation
- ***Choose a text or texts.*** Depending on your students, you might choose a common text for the whole class or unique texts for different groups. Unique texts might be at different Lexile levels or offer different perspectives on a single topic. If time is tight, you may consider giving the text to students to read and annotate ahead of time.
- ***Provide time and quiet to read and annotate.*** Students can read and annotate the text in the large group, before moving into small groups, or after the small groups have assembled. If the class is reading multiple texts, it may be helpful to have students move to their text-specific groups first, then read and annotate. In either case, a quiet classroom is important.
- ***Provide tools for highlighting.*** Make sure each student has a clean, easy-to-read copy of the text and materials with which to annotate it, for example, highlighters, pens, etc. If students cannot write in the text, give them sticky notes for marking their text selections and capturing their comments.

STEPS OF THE PROTOCOL

This version of Save the Last Word for Me has been adapted from the School Reform Initiative website (see Resources). Times provided are guidelines only and can be modified.

1. Introduction (2–3 minutes)
- Facilitator reviews the purposes and the steps of the protocol and offers reminders about any norms that are particularly important.
- Students move into small groups, with a designated facilitator and timekeeper for each group.

2. Highlighting the Text (5–8 minutes, depending on length and complexity of text)
- Students each highlight a passage that, for them, captures or connects to the most significant idea in the text.

3. Presenter Shares (1–2 minutes)
- First presenter identifies the passage she has highlighted as most significant and reads it out loud to the group.
- Presenter says nothing about why she chose that particular passage.

4. Pause for Reflection (1 minute)
- Other students silently reflect on the passage the presenter has shared. They may jot down notes.

5. Participants Share (3–4 minutes)
- Each student except for the presenter has up to 1 minute to respond to the passage, for example, addressing:
  - » What does it make me think about?
  - » What questions does it raise for me?

6. "The Last Word"—Presenter Responds (1–2 minutes)
- Presenter shares why she originally chose that passage, that is, what made her think it was significant?

- Presenter also responds to or builds on what she heard from groupmates about the passage.
- Other participants listen *silently*.

7. Additional Rounds (approximately 7 minutes per round)
- Groups follow the same pattern of presenter reading a passage, other students commenting on it, and presenter offering the last word until all participants in the group have presented and had their own last word.

8. [Optional] Open Discussion (5–7 minutes)
- All students in the group discuss ideas and questions that have emerged during the discussion.

9. Debrief (5–7 minutes)
- Students reflect on how this protocol worked as a tool for exploring ideas in the text and developing their own thinking. Some prompts include:
  » What did I learn from listening to others discuss the passage of text I selected?
  » What did I learn from responding to someone else's text selection?

TIPS FOR FACILITATING THE PROTOCOL

- ***Establish roles.*** Each group should have a facilitator and timekeeper who both participates in and keeps the process moving. In addition, before the rounds begin, groups should establish the presentation order: who will be the first presenter, second, third, etc.
- ***Model passages.*** Make sure students have a good idea of what is meant by a "passage." You might do this by modeling a passage you find significant from another text the class has read recently.
- ***Take a beat.*** Remind students that listening to each other's comments on text selections, as well as the selections themselves, is crucial to their learning. It helps to "take a beat," that is, to pause for a second or two between participants sharing out in the larger group.

SAVE THE LAST WORD FOR ME IN THE CLASSROOM

Barbara Anderson, a teacher at P.S. 42 Benjamin Altman School in New York City, used a scaffolded version of Save the Last Word for Me with her 4th-grade students as part of a research unit on North American explorers. Barbara's goals for the unit were for students to write about the unit's texts using evidence and to make connections to others' ideas about the texts.

Adapting Save the Last Word for Me allowed her to differentiate content by reading level, with groups reading and discussing different texts related to the unit focus. For example, some groups read Eve Spencer's *Three Ships for Columbus* (1993) (a below-reading-level text for her students), and others read Howard Zinn and Rebecca Stefoff's *A Young People's History of the United States* (2007) (an above-reading-level text). For Barbara, when the students' conversations about texts "are more interesting and allow students to have both breadth and depth on a subject, differentiation becomes not only possible but invisible."

To introduce the protocol for the first time and give students time to practice its habits, Barbara had one group of students "fishbowl" one round of the protocol using a text with which they were already familiar. At the end of the round, she asked students outside the fishbowl (those who were observing) to evaluate the conversation during that round, using a discussion rubric with dimensions such as "making connections among ideas" and "extending the group's thinking." She also introduced sentence stems for discussion and had students practice these in small groups. Stems included:

- "I'm wondering _____."
- "Based on my evidence, I think _____."
- "I disagree with _____'s idea, and here's why: _____."

For the full protocol, Barbara divided students into groups of three to four based on the text they had read. She scaffolded each group's discussion about its texts by providing the group with a set of question cards she had prepared. Some of the questions she included were:

- What motivated Columbus to explore?
- In what ways do you think Columbus' exploration of the Americas changed the world?

- What do you imagine the Native Americans thought of Columbus and the European explorers?

After all students had time to read the text, one student became the presenter, who then took the first card from the deck, read the question aloud, and asked her groupmates to respond to it based on what they had read. After everyone had spoken, the presenter had the "last word" on the question, sharing her own ideas and evidence from the text. The presenter then passed the cards to the left, and a new presenter followed the same pattern. It took about 20 minutes for all students to take a turn being the presenter for their group. Finally the students had 5 minutes of open conversation about what they noticed in the text and from the rounds of discussion about the text.

In debriefing the protocol, some students reflected that their initial beliefs about Columbus changed because of the discussion. In terms of the process itself, some felt that 1 minute was too long to share ideas, and others felt it was too short.

For Barbara, Save the Last Word for Me brings equity of voice into her classroom: "So often we have students that tend to dominate discussions, while others we rarely hear from. The protocol makes space for each child to be heard and underscores the importance of hearing others' perspectives."

Barbara modified the protocol by adding guiding questions; typically, students select their passages without such guidance. This scaffolding measure supported the comprehension of her young students and limited student responses of the "I don't know" variety. Barbara valued the ways the protocol helps students to be "flexible in their thinking."

[They] relinquish misconceptions. Revising thinking based upon new evidence is the key to learning. . . . My favorite thing to witness as a teacher is when a child says, "I used to think this about a topic, but after hearing from so and so, my ideas have now changed." The protocol often acts as a cornerstone to developing this flexibility. Students are focusing on listening to each other, then reflect and build on those ideas.

CHAPTER 11

Three Levels of Text

The "rule of three" is a common heuristic for making writing more powerful, funnier, or more satisfying by combining three ideas, examples, questions, etc. (for example, "staying cool, calm, and collected"). Protocol developers at the Southern Maine Partnership at the University of Southern Maine borrowed from the earlier Rule of Three Protocol, developed by Camilla Greene, in creating the Three Levels of Text protocol.

Like the Text Rendering Experience (Chapter 9), Three Levels of Text supports students in entering and deepening their understanding of a text. Also, like that protocol, it specifies how students should respond to the text. However, the two protocols differ in the kinds of responses they invite. While the Text Rendering Experience focuses students exclusively on identifying powerful or compelling elements of the text (specific sentences, phrases, and words), Three Levels of Text asks students not only to identify a meaningful passage (Level 1) but also to interpret the passage (Level 2), and then to identify implications for their own thinking or writing (Level 3). The emphasis on helping students make connections between their reading of a text and their own thinking and writing makes this an ideal protocol for any classroom supporting students to write more effectively (for example, by using mentor texts or in writing their responses to a text).

The second key difference is the order in which students respond to the prompts. In the Text Rendering Experience, all students take a turn responding to just one prompt (for example, identifying a powerful sentence) before the group moves on to the next prompt (identifying a powerful phrase). Three Levels of Text is organized so that each participant responds to all three "levels" (reading a passage, interpreting that passage, and identifying implications of the passage) in the same turn. Of course, Three Levels can be varied so that responses to the three prompts are separated into different rounds.

PURPOSES AND PREPARATION

Purposes
- To deepen understanding of a text
- To collectively make meaning of a text
- To explore connections between the text and students' thinking and writing

Habits Cultivated
- Articulating one's ideas and perspective
- Understanding others' ideas and perspectives

Time
- Typically, 25–40 minutes, including time to read and highlight the text. Time will vary based on the length and complexity of the text and the number of students in each group. In general, plan on about 3–5 minutes per round (which includes all parts of Step 3 below), plus additional time to debrief the protocol.

Preparation
- **Choose the text carefully.** Three Levels of Text tends to work better with texts that are more narrative, imaginative, or poetic than purely informational (such as a set of directions). You might also consider limiting students' focus to a few pages of whatever text they are reading.
- **Give the students the text and the tools they need.** Make sure students have a clean and easily legible copy of the text, preferably one they can underline or highlight. If students cannot write on the text, they can use sticky notes to identify passages and make notes about their thoughts.
- **Make time for reading and thinking.** While the protocol designates time for reading, students may benefit from time to read the text before forming groups. Once in groups, students might take a minute or two to review the text and select the passages they would like to share. In the classroom vignette that follows, Kristen Schaefer uses a graphic organizer to help students do this.

STEPS OF THE PROTOCOL

This version of Three Levels of Text is adapted from the School Reform Initiative website (see Resources). Times provided are guidelines only and can be modified. Each group should have a designated facilitator and timekeeper.

1. Introduction (2–4 minutes)
- Facilitator reviews the purposes for the protocol and the steps involved, as well any guidelines or norms the group has decided upon.

2. Reading and Highlighting (5–10 minutes, depending on length and complexity of text)
- Students read the text and highlight the passages they feel may have implications for or connections to their work.
- While students will only share out one passage that they think is meaningful, encourage students to identify two or three passages. If someone in their group identifies the same passage, then they can switch quickly to a different passage. (Discussions are often richer if the students in a small group each share different passages.)

3. Rounds of Sharing Out (12–20 minutes; approximately 3–5 minutes per participant)
- Each student addresses all three prompts; other students then briefly respond to what that student has said. Students take turns sharing out until everyone in the group has been a presenter.
  - » Level 1: Presenter *reads aloud* a selected passage. (Note: If another participant has previously read the presenter's chosen passage, the presenter should select another one to read.)
  - » Level 2: Presenter says what she *thinks* about the passage (interpreting, connecting to past experiences, etc.).
  - » Level 3: Presenter says what she sees as the *implications* for her work (e.g., her thinking, reading, writing).
  - » Other students in the group respond to what the presenter has said (no more than 2 minutes in total).

[Optional: A group may choose to do more than one go-round, that is, each student may share a second excerpt from the text, explain what she thinks about it, etc.]

4. Debrief (5 minutes)
- Students reflect on the process they have used. Possible prompts include:
  - » How did Three Levels of Text change the way you thought about the text?
  - » What did you learn from what other students shared in their three levels?
  - » How did it (or could it) help you with your writing?
  - » What could make this protocol more helpful to you the next time we do it?

TIPS FOR FACILITATING THE PROTOCOL

- ***Clarify/modify terms.*** Make sure students understand the steps of the protocol, including what is meant by the term *implications*. For example, you might ask students to make connections to their writing or another text they are reading or have read.
- ***Add a round or two.*** The protocol is complete when all students in a group have had a chance to share out all three levels for their selected passage from the text. However, adding a second or third round with the same text encourages students to engage more deeply with the text. Of course, each round takes additional time.
- ***Add time for discussion after rounds.*** It often feels natural to shift into an open discussion following the debrief step. This helps to accommodate different-sized groups, which will take different amounts of time to complete the steps.

THREE LEVELS OF TEXT IN THE CLASSROOM

Kristen Schaefer introduced Three Levels of Text to her 11th-grade English language arts students at Sunset Park High School in Brooklyn, New York, as part of an introductory lesson on Shakespeare's *Macbeth*. The protocol supported students in close reading of a text that provided background information on Shakespeare's life and work. For Kristen, Three Levels of Text provided students with an opportunity "to read, write, and discuss nonfiction texts in preparation for reading a work of literature."

Kristen used a jigsaw-like organization, dividing the class into heterogeneous groups of four. She gave each student within each group a different text excerpt from the same work. She used the discussion prompts (Levels 1, 2, and 3) from the third step of the protocol to create a graphic organizer for students to use in preparing for the discussion. Since Kristen used this protocol to help her students prepare for reading the play, she modified the Level 3 prompt to specify the kinds of implications she wanted students to consider: "Think about the upcoming reading of the play and/or make connections to each other's readings."

After Kristen introduced the purpose for reading, students had 10 minutes to read and write, then 15 minutes for the protocol discussion within their groups. During the protocol portion, each student had 3 minutes to share his or her three "levels." Other students in the group had 2 minutes collectively to respond to what they heard. One student in each group facilitated, making sure that everyone participated; another student kept time for the group. Kristen circulated among the groups as they worked to help them stay on track.

In reflecting on the protocol, Kristen highlighted the benefits of incorporating the graphic organizer, which gave students time to write before sharing out their three levels:

> Having used other text-based protocols with students, it is easy for the discussion to veer off track. I know that my students valued a feeling of preparation, so by adding the writing component, the discussion was enriched.

Having student facilitators allowed Kristen to monitor the groups' work, make any adjustments in timing, and "redirect students on any off-task issues."

While Three Levels of Text is often used with a common text for all students in the class, or at least in the same group, Kristen's jigsaw-style approach supported a rich discussion around a common topic:

> This also added a level of accountability and inherent interest as students were sharing information that was new. It was important that they listen so they could respond and actively participate in the discussion.

CHAPTER 12

Gallery Walk

The definition of literacy has expanded in the 21st century. In addition to more conventional texts students read (on paper or in digital versions), students increasingly engage with and interpret a vast range of other kinds of texts: paintings, photographs, films, songs, blogs, "wikis," websites—even video games.

The Gallery Walk protocol supports students in closely examining multiple texts, often texts with a visual component (e.g., posters, photographs, paintings, maps). Students, typically in small groups, look closely at the texts (sometimes called "exhibits" in this protocol) posted at stations around the room. Usually, their examination is guided by a focus question. Then students discuss their observations, making connections to the focus question.

The Gallery Walk can take just a few minutes or extend to an entire class period. It can also be paired with other protocols, for example, with the Chalk Talk protocol, as in the vignette from Terra Lynch's classroom that follows (see also Chapter 7). It lends itself to a wide range of follow-up activities: small-group discussions, jigsaw discussions, writing assignments, research projects, etc. It can also be used as a way for students to share their own texts with others, in a slightly modified version called the Hosted Gallery Walk (described later in Steps of the Protocol).

The Gallery Walk protocol supports students in reading, writing, and talking about texts of all kinds, helping them deepen a broad range of literacy skills.

PURPOSES AND PREPARATION

Purposes
- To encounter, explore, and interpret texts of all kinds
- To share perspectives on texts with others

Habits Cultivated

- Closely observing and describing
- Articulating one's ideas and perspective
- Making connections to others' ideas and perspectives

Time

- Typically, 25–40 minutes. Time depends on how many stations there are and how long groups spend at each station. A good estimate is 2–4 minutes per station, plus another minute or two for groupmates to share their observations.

Preparation

- ***Organize the space.*** Leave plenty of space in between stations so that groups can comfortably view and discuss the artifact(s) displayed there. Teachers sometimes use the hallway outside their classroom, the school library, or an auditorium. In addition to posters and chart paper, other forms or formats for presenting artifacts are possible, for example, a monitor or laptop for showing a video or website.
- ***Provide materials for viewing and thinking.*** Materials will vary depending on the artifacts (posters, photographs, charts and graphs, etc.) that you want to display. These artifacts are organized into stations: One station might display a single artifact or a group of them. In grouping artifacts at a station, teachers often do so thematically, or in a way that highlights similarities or differences. Clipboards for individual students or a group reporter can be helpful for taking notes as groups circulate among the stations.
- ***Focus viewing and discussion with questions.*** The focus question(s) should relate clearly to the kinds of texts being examined, as well as to the curriculum content and learning objectives. The questions can be identified by the teacher or developed collectively with students. All groups can work with the same question, or each small group might have its own question(s), which allows for a jigsaw discussion following the gallery walk and initial group discussions.
- ***It's all in the details!*** Encourage students to make observations about specific details they notice. Invite them to record their questions, surprises, and insights as well as the similarities and differences they notice among the artifacts in the gallery. Ask them to note also any connections they make with other materials they have previously read and discussed.

STEPS OF THE PROTOCOL

This version of the Gallery Walk is adapted from the School Reform Initiative's Student Work Gallery Walk, the Facing History and Ourselves Gallery Walk, and the EL Education Gallery Walk/Hosted Gallery Walk (see Resources). Times provided are guidelines only and can be modified.

1. Introduction (2–5 minutes)
- Facilitator reviews purposes, steps, and norms for the Gallery Walk.
- Facilitator identifies focus question(s) for viewing the work. (Note: If group decides on the question(s) collectively, add a few minutes to this step.)

2. Station-to-Station (10–20 minutes, depending on number of stations)
- Groups rotate from station to station, as directed by facilitator.
- At each station, students examine and make notes about the artifacts displayed there. (Students might make notes on clipboards or on sticky notes provided at the stations).
- Facilitator (or timekeeper) calls time after 2–4 minutes at a station.

3. Group Discussions (5 minutes)
- Groups meet to discuss their observations and questions from all the stations and how these relate to the focus question(s). For example:
  - » A detail that I noticed was . . .
  - » I was surprised to see . . .
  - » One connection I can make between two artifacts is . . .
  - » A question I have from Station 2 is . . . ?

4. Reporting Out (5–8 minutes)
- Reporter from each group shares out ideas (themes, questions, patterns, etc.) identified by their group.
- [Optional: Recorder captures ideas from the reports on chart paper or projected document.]

5. Debrief (5 minutes)

- Participants reflect on the experience of doing the Gallery Walk. Possible questions for the debrief include:
  - » What is most challenging or interesting to me about "reading" texts this way?
  - » How did working with my groupmates support my learning?
  - » What can we do differently next time to make the Gallery Walk more effective?

Hosted Gallery Walk variation: In this version, students present work they have created individually or collaboratively. Such work might include posters, maps, model designs, or multimedia presentations. During Step 2: Station-to-Station, the creator(s) of the work may stand beside the work to introduce it and answer questions about it. For this version, it helps to extend the time for this step and organize it so that students who have created work can also visit other stations and interact with the creators of the pieces displayed there.

TIPS FOR FACILITATING THE PROTOCOL

- ***Establish norms for viewing and talking.*** While observing closely is the main activity of Step 2: Station-to-Station, students often learn from sharing observations with a groupmate. To help guide these informal conversations, develop and review norms with students before they begin rotating from station to station. Helpful norms might include: students *silently* observe the artifacts at the station for at least 2 minutes before quietly talking with one another; keep conversation focused on the artifacts and the focus question; etc.
- ***"You can observe a lot by watching."*** Yogi Berra's famous quip reminds us that learning from observation takes time. Like many of us, students may be used to glancing quickly at an image and then moving on to the next. Encourage students to spend a good amount of time at each station observing quietly before making notes or discussing it with groupmates. You might need to help them by timing a period of silence at the beginning of each rotation and letting students know when it is okay to talk.

- *Emphasize description, not evaluation.* Encourage students to begin by describing the artifacts, paying attention to details, and then perhaps raising questions about it. Direct students to hold off on making a judgment about what they like or don't like. You can practice this with students before the protocol by asking them to observe an object (something on the wall or on the teacher's desk) for 30 seconds and then inviting them to describe it as concretely and specifically as possible. After sharing their observations, the students can determine which are truly descriptions and which may be evaluations or judgments.

GALLERY WALK IN THE CLASSROOM

When Terra Lynch (a co-author of this book) was teaching 10th-grade humanities at University Neighborhood High School in New York City, as much as half of her class was composed of English language learners; in addition, many of the native English speakers read below grade level. Terra used the Gallery Walk protocol at the beginning of a unit on colonialism and power. She wanted to help students develop the knowledge and vocabulary they would need to engage with the content of the unit, as well as to support students' understanding of how to examine and interpret images. She combined the Gallery Walk with elements of the Chalk Talk protocol (see Chapter 7).

Terra selected images related to the Opium Wars from the period of the British Empire, including photographs of a poppy flower and an opium den, a map representing the opium trade, a political cartoon from the era, and others. At five separate stations around the room, she posted each artifact on a piece of chart paper. Terra gave the groups this focus for their gallery walk: "Write down anything interesting, a question, or a prediction about how the image relates to the topic of colonialism." Borrowing a component from the Chalk Talk, she encouraged students to use markers to write a reply or draw images directly on the chart paper itself.

For about 20 minutes (approximately 4 minutes per station), groups circulated among the stations, looking closely at the images and making comments on the chart paper. Terra then distributed the chart papers among the groups and asked groups to identify any patterns they noticed in the comments on the sheet they were given.

After 6–7 minutes, a spokesperson from each group shared out a pattern or patterns the group had identified; for example: "We noticed on this page, there are a lot of questions about what kind of plant this is. Nobody made a prediction about colonialism." Terra then asked them to "look across the posters and notes" for any patterns. Students shared these out in the large group; for example: "All have to do with colonialism in Asia." Terra took notes during the share out.

Terra reflected on the power of this protocol, especially for English language learners who struggle with the vocabulary demands of texts related to the topic: "Students really responded to the power of visuals. It can be so eye opening for them." She recalled one student, Roberto, seeing the photograph of the opium smoker in the opium den, saying, "What? I can't believe we're learning about this in school!" Even after the activity, the images continued to serve as a learning resource. "I hung the images on the wall during the unit," Terra reported, "so students and I could refer to them continuously."

The Gallery Walk works well for several reasons, according to Terra: "It 'front loads' knowledge so that students have something 'sticky' to which they can connect new information. It gives them something concrete to focus on first, and then we can move into the theoretical." The protocol also gives students practice asking and answering each other's questions in a low-stakes environment. "Finally," Terra shares, "it gets students physically moving around the classroom, which helps keep the teenagers alert and engaged—especially after lunch!"

CHAPTER 13

Ladder of Feedback

The Ladder of Feedback was developed by David Perkins and colleagues at Harvard Project Zero. Like the Tuning Protocol (Chapter 14), the Ladder of Feedback recognizes that meaningful feedback rarely occurs spontaneously. Instead, participants in a feedback process—those giving and those receiving—benefit from a structure that encourages feedback that is focused, specific, and multidimensional (that is, not focused only on praise or suggestions).

The Ladder of Feedback, like many protocols, asks participants to resist the natural impulse to begin with offering suggestions. Instead, it puts a premium on helping the group get clear about what the work-in-progress is trying to accomplish before trying to "fix" it. This requires what David Perkins has described as "communicative feedback":

> Communicative feedback clarifies the idea or behavior under consideration, so that everyone is talking about the same thing. It communicates positive features so that they can be preserved and built on. It communicates concerns and suggestions toward improvement. (2003, p. 46)

The Ladder of Feedback can be used with works-in-progress in many forms, including drafts, outlines or plans, and visual art, as described in the classroom vignette. The most important factor in deciding whether to use the Ladder of Feedback is whether the creator of the work is ready for and open to feedback on her work.

The heart of the Ladder of Feedback is the group's progression through a series of steps up the "ladder," from getting clear on what the presenter is working on to identifying strengths about the work, to raising concerns, and finally to offering suggestions. After the clarifying step, the presenter listens but does not respond to the feedback. In climbing the ladder, students practice important skills and habits that make offering and receiving feedback a more powerful learning experience in other contexts, including peer-editing, offering written feedback on a draft, and others.

PURPOSES AND PREPARATION

Purposes
- To provide informed and constructive feedback on a work-in-progress
- To learn about one another's work

Habits Cultivated
- Giving balanced, specific feedback
- Resisting the impulse to leap to judgments or suggestions

Time
- Typically, 25–35 minutes. The protocol can be completed in as little as 10 minutes, but it typically takes at least 20 minutes, depending on the nature of the work being examined, the size of the group, and other factors.

Preparation
- **Check-in with presenter.** Preparation for the Ladder of Feedback is less extensive than preparation for the Tuning Protocol (Chapter 14); in fact, the Ladder can be used on the spur of the moment. However, the facilitator might still want to check in briefly with the presenter ahead of time to make sure she knows what work she will present for feedback and understands the steps of the protocol. In some cases, the presenter may have a specific focus for feedback to share with the group, but this is not required.
- **Define "feedback."** You might want to review and even practice some of the qualities of effective feedback with students before the protocol. Students often need extra encouragement to be specific in their feedback (stating specifically what it is in the work that leads to their questions, concerns, etc.) and to keep the focus on the work, not the creator.
- **Provide materials.** All students should have easy access to the work being presented as well as to any criteria the presenter might have used in producing it, for example, a rubric or a checklist.

STEPS OF THE PROTOCOL

This version of the Ladder of Feedback has been adapted from *King Arthur's Round Table* by David Perkins (see References). Times included are guidelines only and can be modified.

1. Introduction (2–4 minutes)
- Facilitator reviews the purposes and the steps of the protocol, as well as any guidelines or norms the group has agreed upon.

2. Presentation (3–5 minutes)
- Presenter shares the work-in-progress. (Note: Presenter may share a specific focus for feedback, but this is not required.)

3. Clarify (3–5 minutes)
- Participants ask clarifying questions to make sure they understand the work-in-progress. (Note: Facilitator should advise students to avoid offering suggestions or evaluations "disguised" as clarifying questions.)
- Presenter answers each question as concisely as possible.

4. Value (3–5 minutes)
- Students express what they like about the work-in-progress, for example, specific elements that they think work well. (Note: Facilitator should remind students to be specific in pointing out what they value in the work.)
- Presenter listens *silently*.

5. State Concerns (3–5 minutes)
- Students state their puzzles and concerns about the work-in-progress. (Note: Facilitator might advise students to avoid absolutes, for example, "What's wrong is . . . ," and instead to use qualified terms, such as, "I wonder if . . ." "It seems to me . . ." etc.)
- Presenter listens *silently*.

6. Suggest (3–5 minutes)
- Students suggest things the presenter might do to improve the work. (Note: Facilitator may choose to blend this step with Step

3: Concerns, since people often state concerns and then offer suggestions for addressing them.)
- Presenter listens *silently*.

7. Presenter Reflects (1–2 minutes)
- Presenter may briefly comment on one or two things she heard in the feedback discussion that help her think about her work-in-progress. (Note: Facilitator should remind presenter not to defend or offer further explanations of her work.)

8. Debrief (approximately 5 minutes)
- Students reflect on what was effective about the protocol, how it might be improved, and how the group might use it in the future. (Note: Facilitator may give the presenter the option to comment first on how the discussion was helpful to her.)

TIPS FOR FACILITATING THE PROTOCOL

- ***Take the steps slowly!*** Even if the group is doing the protocol in 10 or 15 minutes, try to make sure that the group does not rush through the steps of clarifying and valuing in order to get to concerns and suggestions. This may mean asking the group to slow down, look again at the work-in-progress, or pair–share with a neighbor.
- ***Model it.*** Depending on a group's familiarity and comfort with the Ladder of Feedback and similar protocols, participants may need examples at the beginning of—or even during—one or more steps to know how to gauge their own participation in a particular step. After modeling a specific kind of feedback, step back and let the students do the work.
- ***Get it write.*** It is often helpful to build in time for brief writing before each step, or even just one of the steps. For example, "Take a minute and jot down one or two concerns you have. What about the work-in-progress is leading to this concern?"
- ***Remind the presenter to listen.*** It may be challenging for the presenter to just listen to the feedback without adding information, explaining, or defending the work. Remind the presenter that the feedback belongs to her, and she can let go of

anything that is off the mark: "Focus on those things that get you thinking about your work and how it might be strengthened."

LADDER OF FEEDBACK IN THE CLASSROOM

Beth Hansen, a middle school art teacher at Quaboag Regional Middle/ High School in Warren, Massachusetts, had always believed it was important for students to give feedback to one another on their art-work. Going beyond simply creating to reflecting on and analyzing their own and others' work was, she felt, an important opportunity for students to deepen their understanding of the art concepts and techniques at the core of her curriculum.

However, getting students to engage productively in this kind of feedback had been challenging. The few times she had asked students to try giving feedback to one another, they had either said very little or had talked in such vague generalities that the feedback simply wasn't helpful to the students: No one had a clear direction when it came time to revise their work.

Learning about the Ladder of Feedback at a professional develop-ment session (where it was used as a tool for teachers to give feedback to one another on unit plans), Beth decided to give it a try in her class-room. As students neared the completion of a first draft of the draw-ings they were working on, she called for a pause in the work so that she could explain the process they were about to use. "The steps of the Ladder are pretty simple—they got it right away," Beth reported.

Given that it was the students' first time using a protocol, she de-cided to set up the protocol as a whole-class discussion that she would facilitate. In addition to providing students with copies of the Ladder of Feedback, she posted in the classroom the criteria that she wanted them to focus on most closely: composition, color, and others. Beth asked five students who had completed their drafts to post their work on the walls. To help the presenters focus on what they were hear-ing, she encouraged them to take notes while their piece was being discussed so that they would be able to refer to the feedback in the revision process.

Then, beginning with the first piece, Beth guided the class through the steps of the protocol. "They needed a little reminding at first to do one step at a time. Students sometimes like to say things like, 'I like the way you did this, but you need to improve that.' I had to remind them that in the Ladder of Feedback, we keep those two things separate." The class spent about 10 minutes on each piece.

Once the students had the hang of it, Beth said, "it worked like a charm." The Ladder of Feedback provided the structure, the criteria helped to keep students focused on substance, and they were able to generate useful feedback for their peers in short order.

In the succeeding class periods, Beth divided the students' time between art making and critique using the Ladder of Feedback, rotating through the remainder of the students' work over the course of a few days. Doing so allowed student artists to experience the power of offering informed feedback as well as receiving it.

CHAPTER 14

Tuning Protocol

The Tuning Protocol was developed by Joseph McDonald and colleagues at the Coalition of Essential Schools in the early 1990s as a tool for teachers to provide one another with informed and useful feedback on an assignment, a task, or an assessment. The group helps the presenter "fine-tune" the work so that it is clearer, stronger, and more effective when it is used again with students—Joe used the analogy of tuning a piano or a radio dial (from the days when people listened to radios with dials!).

The protocol creates a safe space for a group to offer both *warm* (affirming) and *cool* (questioning) feedback on the presenter's work. Crucially, in the Tuning Protocol, as in several other protocols, the presenter does not respond to questions or offer more information during the warm and cool feedback. Instead, she has the rare opportunity to listen in as colleagues discuss her work. When the presenter does speak again, she reflects on just one or two of the ideas, questions, and/or suggestions that emerged in the feedback discussion.

In addition to its value in the classroom, the Tuning Protocol has been used in other settings as a way of supporting students in critiquing one another's work. For example, the Education Video Center in New York City has long used the protocol to structure peer-critique on student-created documentaries. According to founder Steve Goodman, using the Tuning Protocol "ensures the positive parts are identified as well as the areas that need improvement. Hearing what worked well helps the students be more open to hearing the critical feedback about what needs to be strengthened." Steve also points to the value of students facilitating protocols. "It gives them a sense of ownership over the critique process."

PURPOSES AND PREPARATION

Purposes
- To provide informed and constructive feedback on a work-in-progress
- To learn about one another's work

Habits Cultivated
- Identifying specific evidence
- Sharing one's ideas and perspective
- Understanding others' ideas and perspectives

Time
- Typically, 25–35 minutes. Times may be adjusted to accommodate different kinds of work-in-progress presented, as well as the number of participants.

Preparation
- ***Preconference with presenter.*** This brief meeting with the presenter before the protocol, which could be earlier in the class period or during a prior class meeting, is essential. The facilitator needs to understand the work that the presenter will present for feedback and the kinds of feedback she would like to get. The facilitator helps the presenter develop a focusing question for feedback (for example, "How could I use personal examples more effectively in my essay?" "What parts of the podcast are most and least compelling? Why?"). If students are serving as facilitators, include them in this preconference.
- ***Make the work visible.*** Whatever the format of the student work that is being "tuned," make sure it is easily visible and accessible to all participants. This can be done by making copies, putting the work in the center of the table so participants can see it, posting it on walls, projecting it on a Smart Board or monitor, or other solutions.

STEPS OF THE PROTOCOL

This version of the Tuning Protocol is adapted from *The Power of Protocols* and *Looking Together at Student Work* (see Resources). Times provided are guidelines only and can be modified.

1. Introduction (2 minutes)
- Facilitator briefly introduces protocol purposes, roles, steps, and norms.

2. Presentation (3–5 minutes)
- Presenter provides context for the work to be "tuned," which might include:
  - » What is the assignment, task, or prompt for the work?
  - » What are the presenter's goals for the work? (These may relate to learning objectives, standards, or personal hopes and aspirations.)
  - » What was the process used to create it? (research, group collaboration, stages, etc.)
  - » How is the work assessed? (rubric, checklist, etc.)
- Presenter offers a focusing question for feedback.
- Other students listen *silently*.

3. Clarifying Questions (2–4 minutes)
- Facilitator invites brief informational questions to better understand the context for the work (e.g., "How long did it take to make this?" "Did you work alone or with a group?")
- Presenter answers each briefly. (Note: Facilitator should suggest that any questions that are not actually clarifying be saved for the Warm & Cool Feedback step to come.)

4. Examining Work Sample (approximately 5 minutes, depending on nature of work)
- Students look closely at the work with the presenter's focusing question in mind.
- Students think about comments, observations, questions, etc., they would like to offer as warm and cool feedback; they may jot these down.

5. Warm & Cool Feedback (5–10 minutes)
- Students share warm and cool feedback with each other, trying to connect feedback to presenter's focusing question as much as possible. Facilitator reminds group of difference between warm and cool, and typically invites warm comments first:
  - » *Warm* feedback includes observations and comments about ways in which the work meets its goals and other strengths.

> » *Cool* feedback includes probing questions, possible gaps between the work and its goals, and suggestions.
- Presenter listens *silently.*

6. Reflection (2–3 minutes)
- Presenter reflects on comment(s) or question(s) that have stimulated her thinking about revising or improving the work. (Note: Facilitator may remind presenter to focus on just one or two: "Don't try to answer everybody's question or comment.")
- Other students listen *silently.*

7. Debrief (5 minutes)
- All students reflect on their individual experiences during the protocol, as well as suggestions for how it could be improved next time. (Facilitator may give presenter option of going first.)

TIPS FOR FACILITATING THE PROTOCOL

- ***Begin with a volunteer.*** Carole Colburn, whose classroom is profiled in this chapter, suggests having students volunteer to be the presenters in the class's first Tuning Protocols. "I recommend introducing the process first to the whole class and then, in advance, asking a student or two who you know will be comfortable going first. Once students see how great the process is, others will want to have their own work 'tuned.'"
- ***Clarify "clarifying."*** It can be tricky for students to keep clarifying questions focused on getting the contextual information rather than offering feedback (typically suggestions or critique) in the guise of clarifying questions. For example, "How long did you work on the first draft?" is a clarifying question. "Did you try beginning your essay with your concluding paragraph?" is most likely a suggestion disguised as a question, and belongs in the Warm & Cool Feedback step.
- ***Model warm and cool feedback.*** Students may practice with offering warm feedback, which identifies specific strengths in the work, as well as cool feedback, which points to possible gaps and raises questions. Remind students that the feedback is focused on the work, not the creator. (For example, cool feedback might be phrased, "I am a bit confused by how this essay begins . . .").

Carole Colburn, the teacher in the vignette that follows, found it helpful to suggest that her students begin cool feedback with phrases such as "I wonder if . . ." or "I noticed that . . ."

- **Begin with warm.** The facilitator should encourage students to share some of their warm comments first before moving to invite cool (or "cooler" comments). Doing so generally allows the presenter to relax and listen more attentively to both warm and cool feedback.
- **Let the presenter be "selfish."** Presenters, whatever their age, often want to answer all the questions and respond to all the comments that come up in the feedback—a generous impulse, but one that can lead to superficial reflections. Suggest instead that the presenter reflect aloud on just one or two questions or comments that got her thinking the most. The goal is not to answer all the group's questions or to solve all the problems but to begin a process of thinking about and working on them.

TUNING PROTOCOL IN THE CLASSROOM

Carole Colburn, a teacher at the Highlander Way Middle School, in Howell, Michigan, described using the Tuning Protocol with her 7th-grade communication arts classes on a five-paragraph persuasive essay assignment. She gave students several prompts to choose from, most asking students to choose a position to argue for or against in order to convince the reader. Example prompts included: "Kids should be given an allowance from their parents or not" and "Using online communication tools such as email and various social media is either helpful to people or not so helpful."

Carole's primary goal in using the Tuning Protocol was to support students in improving their writing skills through peer feedback. In addition, she wanted her students to "appreciate the value of both giving and receiving feedback, and the value of having their work assessed by others whose only purpose is to help them to get better at writing."

Carole facilitated the first protocol with one girl presenting her essay draft in the large group. Carole found that it was particularly important, early on, to model for students some ways of offering feedback, for example, beginning a cool comment or question with "I wonder if . . ." or "I noticed that . . ." "Once the first student had presented and received feedback," Carole reports, "several other students asked to have their work 'tuned.'"

Carole created two smaller groups (of about eight to nine students each) to go through the protocol. In each of these groups, students served as facilitators and timekeepers. Carole pointed out how effective it was for her to model facilitation first: "After students saw how I facilitated the protocol, they caught on very quickly. . . . They really got into it—once they saw how it worked, more students were eager to share their work." One student commented:

> Being a participant in the Tuning Protocol to review someone else's work made me feel comfortable. I like editing and correcting thoughts and ideas that were not my own. It felt comfortable to give the speaker warm feedback. When I give them warm feedback, I know that I am praising them, and their feelings will not get hurt.

Another student recognized the value of giving both warm and cool feedback:

> When giving warm feedback, I found that it felt nice to be making some other person more confident with their work. However, when giving cool feedback, I felt like I was helping the person with constructive criticism.

Carole and her class spent five class periods doing the Tuning Protocol. Even so, not all students presented their work and received feedback. Carole reflected on how she could integrate Tuning Protocols as a regular component of her class:

> I think all students should have the chance to have at least some of their work tuned throughout the year. Perhaps I could find one day a week or perhaps every other week where students could work in smaller groups to run this protocol.

Carole also recognized the value of students becoming facilitators of the protocol:

> I could also imagine a scenario, once students understood the protocol, where they could easily run it themselves, and I would set up two to three smaller groups so that multiple students would have the chance each time to have their work "tuned."

Part III

GETTING BETTER
WITH PROTOCOLS

CHAPTER 15

Getting the Most Out of the Debrief

The debrief is the last step of each protocol in this book—and of many, many other protocols not included here. In the debrief, students shift their attention from the topic, question, or text they have been discussing to the process of the protocol itself. In the typical debrief, students reflect on questions such as, "What was it like to use the protocol?" "What went well?" or "What was challenging for you?"

While usually quick and informal in nature, the debrief is an important opportunity for students' learning. It supports students (and the teacher) in deepening their understanding of:

- The protocol as a tool, including when and how to use it
- Themselves as learners and collaborators, including the particular skills and habits needed to engage productively with complex questions and topics as well as with others' perspectives on those topics
- The class as a learning community, including the important differences among classmates and the power of multiple perspectives on complex questions, topics, texts, and pieces of students' work

Addressing these issues explicitly and openly in the debrief makes it more likely that students will develop important habits and skills that protocols rely upon and enable students to practice. It also encourages students to transfer these habits and skills to other contexts both inside and outside the classroom.

In this chapter, we offer some questions often used to initiate the debrief. We also identify challenges groups may encounter in the debrief step and share some ideas for addressing them.

QUESTIONS FOR DEBRIEFING PROTOCOLS

Given the brevity of debriefs, you probably won't have time to invite student reflections on all the questions you would like to. Instead, decide on one or two issues that you feel are most important to the class's learning, and focus on these. You might try including a question or two about the group's work together (such as the first and last questions that follow) and one or two questions about students' individual experiences or learning. Using pairs or clusters of related questions (such as those in the following list) encourages students to elaborate on their experiences and perspectives.

Here are some possible questions:

- What was the purpose of this protocol? How well do you think we achieved it as a group?
- What skills or habits did you practice in this protocol? What do you feel you did well? What do you need to work on?
- Which steps in this protocol seemed especially helpful or important to you? Why? Which steps were puzzling to you or difficult for you? Why?
- In what other situations might this protocol be useful? Which steps of this protocol could you imagine using in other situations?
- What if we had had this conversation without a protocol? How might it have been different?
- If we did this protocol again, what would make it more useful? What should we keep the same, and what should we try to do differently?

Students, especially younger ones, may find it easier to respond to questions with a sentence starter. Any of these questions can be framed as a sentence stem that students can complete—for example, "The most helpful step of this protocol for me was _____ because _____."

CHALLENGES IN DEBRIEFING PROTOCOLS

While the debrief step may seem straightforward on paper, in practice, it presents a few challenges. Here are some of those challenges as well as ideas for meeting them.

Challenge: Reserving Time for the Debrief

Debriefs are usually short, 5 minutes on average. Beginner groups might benefit from a longer debrief, while experienced groups can often do an effective debrief in 2–3 minutes. Finding even 2 or 3 minutes in the jam-packed day of the classroom can feel like a colossal challenge. Here are some suggestions for holding that time:

- *Estimate times before the protocol starts.* Many protocols have pre-established times for each step, which you'll likely need to adapt for your own context.
- *Be the timer.* Whether you are facilitating the protocol for the whole group, or circulating through the room as students facilitate small groups, it can be easy to get caught up in the moment and to lose track of time. Try setting a timer to help you stay on top of it. Let students know when there is a minute left in a step to give them time to prepare for the shift.
- *Do the debrief the next day.* Even with your best efforts, protocols sometimes run overtime, and the debrief gets squeezed out. If this happens, try starting the next class meeting with a reflection on the protocol that was carried out in the previous class. While something might be lost in terms of the immediacy of students' reflections, doing a debrief at the beginning of a class period means that the students are fresher and more focused than they might be at the end of the protocol. You can also suggest students write some brief reflections as homework.

Challenge: Focusing on the Process of the Protocol

When protocols are working well, they foster deep engagement in the questions, issues, texts, or samples of student work being discussed. At the end of the protocol, students may well feel as though they're not finished sharing ideas or giving feedback. Shifting gears to the debrief can be a challenge. Here are some strategies that can help:

- *Explain the purpose of the debrief.* Help students make the cognitive shift to a different kind of discussion by taking a few seconds at the start of the debrief to explain its purpose and importance. For example:

We've been having a really good and intense conversation about [this issue/text/questions/etc.]. You might even feel like you've got a lot more to say about those ideas. That's great! We'll be coming back to those ideas in a later class, but now we have another task. When we talk to each other using a protocol, we're practicing some important habits: carefully listening to each other and asking good questions, etc. The protocol is a tool that helps us get better at these skills. If we want to learn to use the tool more effectively, we need to step back and think about how well it is working and what we need to do to get better at it. That's what we're going to do in this debrief step.

- **Give students time to make notes about additional ideas or questions they have.** Right before the debrief step, it might be helpful to announce to students that the conversation is about to shift. Invite 1 minute of quiet reflection so that they can write down (or capture in some other form) any last ideas or questions about the topic, the question, or the text that they want to remember. Let them know that they are writing these ideas down because the group will not be talking about them in the next step, and you want to make sure they have a way of remembering things they might want to come back to in a subsequent class period. Using a 2-minute Turn & Talk (see Chapter 3) can help students think about what they might want to record. You can also collect what students write and use it as a resource for planning future lessons (but let them know ahead of time that you plan to do this).
- **Invite students to put away the work or the text they have been discussing.** If the protocol you have been using involves discussing a particular text or examining student work, at the start of the debrief, you can invite students to put it away and to focus instead on the hard copy of the protocol. You might start this process by saying (or by inviting the student facilitators to say):

Okay, everyone, now we're going to shift into our debrief. We stop talking about the question [or text or topic] that we have been discussing and instead focus on the protocol itself—the process of our discussion and how effectively we carried it out. So, to signal that we're shifting gears, would you please turn the work [or text] that you've been discussing face down on the desk [or hand it back to the presenter], and put your copy of the protocol face up where you can refer to it easily.

Challenge: Sharing Perspectives/Feelings/Experiences Openly

Especially early in the school year, or when the group is new to protocols, some students might find it challenging to share their reflections openly and genuinely. Several factors might play into this. A student might be worried about being the only one who struggled with a step or who didn't understand the purpose of the conversation. Conversely, students might be equally worried about being the only one who understood or really enjoyed the protocol when others seemed to struggle with it.

Students might simply be unused to being asked to share their personal reflections in class, wondering if there is a "right answer" that they should provide. If students have been working in small groups, they might be concerned about sounding critical of their peers. On the other hand, some students might actually be critical of their peers and attempt to use the debrief step to complain about the way others participated. Here are some strategies to help students to reflect honestly and constructively:

- *Give students a little time to think quietly before inviting responses.* There are a number of questions that you might use to frame the debrief (such as those mentioned previously). Pose the question (or invite the student facilitators to pose the question) and then allow a little time (anywhere from 15 seconds to a minute) for students to think quietly about their responses. (They might or might not choose to make notes.) Then invite reflections out loud.
- *Decide whether to debrief as a class, in small groups, or some combination.* For students who might be reluctant to speak in the whole group, asking them to share their thoughts in small groups might be more comfortable. On the other hand, you might feel the need to guide the debriefing process more carefully (especially with students learning about what a debrief is). In this case, you might want to do the debrief as a

whole-class discussion facilitated by you. Many teachers find a combination is helpful—have students talk in pairs or small groups for a few minutes, then invite comments out loud in the whole group.

- **Model some of your own perspectives and experiences.** It can be helpful for students, especially in early uses of protocols (and debriefs) to hear you share some of your own genuine reflections on being part of this discussion.

- **Allow students to share reflections anonymously.** Post the debrief question and give the students index cards on which to write a short response. Have the students drop the index cards into a small box or bag, and then draw a few of them out to read out loud to the class. If you feel that you should keep an eye on the kinds of comments that are shared, then you should be the person to draw and read. Otherwise, you can mix up the index cards, hand them back out to the class, and have students read aloud the (anonymous) comments.

- **Check in with presenters and facilitators.** For those protocols with a presenter, such as the Ladder of Feedback (Chapter 13) and the Tuning Protocol (Chapter 14), presenters often spend time sitting quietly during the protocol, listening to the group's feedback. In the debrief, you might want to turn to the presenter(s) first and ask, "What was it like to share your work in this process?" Similarly, inviting student facilitators to share reflections on what was challenging about their role can help to build the class's understanding of protocol facilitation. (You might then ask other students to identify "moves," or specific things the facilitator said and did, that helped them take part in the protocol.)

- **Invite students to reflect on both their individual participation, as well as how the group worked.** Invite the students to fill out a "four-square" reflection: a graphic organizer in which they identify what they themselves did well in the protocol and what they struggled with, as well as what they think the group did well and what the group struggled with (see Figure 15.1).

Figure 15.1. Four-Square Reflection

	Did Well	Need to Improve
Me		
Us		

Getting better at debriefing protocols is itself a developmental process—for teachers as well as for their students. If something did not work well in the debrief step for one protocol, think about—and ask students to think about—what might help the next one go better.

CHAPTER 16

Documenting and Deepening the Learning

A single protocol can be an engaging and powerful learning experience for students, but how do teachers make protocol-guided discussions an essential part of classroom learning? How can they make sure that the ideas, questions, and skills developed in the protocol feed students' ongoing development and thinking? Responses to these questions lie in two strategies that should accompany the use of protocols in the classroom:

- Documenting the learning and reflections that students do during and at the end of protocols
- Using that documentation in the classroom to engage or re-engage students with their ideas, questions, and reflections to deepen student learning

In the sections that follow, we offer suggestions for each of these two important approaches to maximizing students' learning through protocols.

DOCUMENTING STUDENT LEARNING IN PROTOCOLS

Protocols are largely about discussion, and while a lot of learning can happen through discussion, it can feel ephemeral. Discussions (even protocol-guided discussions) move swiftly, and it is often hard to remember after the fact exactly what was said and who said it. In this section, we offer strategies for capturing not only what happens in a protocol but also what the students are learning. The list begins with the simplest and most efficient (especially in terms of time) and concludes with somewhat more involved strategies.

- *Invite all students to write as well speak during the debrief.*
In the previous chapter, we suggested a few debriefing
techniques that involve writing: Have students write a
response to the debrief questions on index cards or invite
students to fill out a "four-square" reflection form. If your
school uses tablets or laptops, these reflections can be
submitted online. Be sure to collect these reflections, whether
done electronically or on hard copy. That way, you can review
the thinking of all students, not just those who spoke during
the discussion. Be sure to share with students some of what
you collect (see the next section for ideas about how to do
this).

- *Invite students to write about the content of the protocol
as well as the process.* This can be a little tricky if you do it
during the debrief. After all, the debrief proper is about the
process of the protocol, not the content of the discussion.
If you open up reflection on content at this point, there
is a good chance that the group may be drawn back into
discussing the question, topic, text, or student work sample(s)
rather than reflecting on the process of the protocol and their
learning. Consider these other ways of capturing students'
content-specific ideas and questions that emerge during the
protocol:
  » At the end of each protocol step, allow 30 seconds of quiet
    for reflective writing. Invite students to write down one
    idea that they want to remember. They might also write
    down a quote (or paraphrased quote) from a classmate
    that seemed especially important to them.
  » After the penultimate step of the protocol and before
    the debrief, give students time to write briefly using the
    Insight/Question (I/Q) strategy: one insight they have
    gained about the topic or about the assignment being
    reviewed and one question they now have. Have them put
    their names on these and turn them in.

- *Take photographs and invite students to write captions.* If
the students are working in small groups to carry out the
protocols, take photographs of the groups as they work. (Make
sure you let students know why you are photographing
them.) Print a few and bring a few copies to class the next day.
Ask students to look at the photographs of their particular

groups (or of the class as a whole) and to write a caption that
answers questions such as: "What kinds of learning were going
on here? Why do I think so?"

- **Use a recording device to capture portions of the discussion.**
  This is probably the most labor intensive of these suggestions,
  though the payoff can be significant in terms of student
  learning. Focusing on either a whole-class protocol or one
  or more small-group protocols, run a recording device (a
  smartphone or tablet app is usually fine). Then choose a small
  portion (2–5 minutes) to play back for students the next time
  they meet. (A rough transcription can help, though it is not
  necessary.) Choose a portion in which particularly complex
  ideas are being discussed or one that illustrates particular
  strengths of the group as they engage in protocol-guided
  discussion. Ask the students to reflect on and write about the
  learning that they think is happening and any new ideas it
  gives them about either the topic and/or how to participate in
  protocol-guided discussions.

USING DOCUMENTATION TO DEEPEN LEARNING

Unused documentation artifacts mostly just contribute to classroom
clutter. To support ongoing learning, the documentation needs to be
used by both you and the students. Here are some strategies for re-
launching discussions, refining questions, identifying areas of challenge, and working on those challenges:

- **Share and discuss quotes from student reflections.** After
  collecting any brief reflective writing that students have done
  (during or at the end of the protocol), compile some or all
  quotations (anonymously, if you wish) in a document and
  print it out for students. If these quotations are focused on the
  process of the protocol, you might review them with students
  just prior to doing the next protocol. If the comments are
  about the content of the discussion, you might use them to
  launch the next day's discussion of that topic. Invite students
  to read through the reflections and identify those that catch
  their attention or raise questions for them.

- *Create a presentation using quotations from student reflections and photographs from the protocol.* Using PowerPoint, Prezi, or another presentation tool, project students' quotes, photographs you took of students at work, and other artifacts from the protocols. Let the presentation run as students are coming into class. At the beginning of class, ask students to identify quotations or photos that particularly caught their attention and say why.
- *Use a Gallery Walk.* Post photographs and quotations from a protocol-guided discussion (or series of protocols) around the classroom. Using the Gallery Walk protocol (Chapter 12), invite students (usually in groups) to walk around and review the photos and quotes and to make connections between the artifacts and that day's class discussion or activity. This can be done in the next class, a few days later, or even weeks after the protocol was conducted.
- *Share reflections across classes.* If you teach multiple classes of the same grade/subject, you might compile reflections from across the classes to share with all students. This can be especially helpful when you have a class or two that is particularly strong in, or particularly challenged by, protocol-guided discussion. Sometimes being able to see and discuss the reflections of peers who have had a very different experience can be helpful.
- *Create student documentation teams.* Students can also take turns carrying out many of these documentation roles: photographing peers at work, reading through their peers' quotations and selecting some to share with the class, creating presentations of photos and quotes that capture what to them seemed most essential about the learning, and so on. Putting students in charge of documentation only amplifies the opportunities for learning.

Carefully documenting students' experiences with protocols and thoughtfully using that documentation opens powerful avenues for deepening and extending their learning.

CHAPTER 17

Troubleshooting During the Protocol

Protocols help students have a thoughtful and substantive discussion about a particular question, topic, text, or sample of student work. Used well, protocols also support students in developing essential skills and habits for discussion and collaboration. They cultivate a level of self-awareness that helps students both inside and outside of school. But these added benefits develop only over time and only if students are encouraged to use protocols rigorously and thoughtfully.

In this chapter, we outline common challenges that students experience as they develop facility with protocols and suggest strategies that you (or student facilitators) might use to address these challenges.

CHALLENGE: SOME STUDENTS ARE TALKING A LOT— OTHERS, NOT AT ALL

The goal of using a protocol is rarely to have all students speak exactly the same amount, but rather to encourage all students to participate thoughtfully and actively in the discussion. Here are some strategies for addressing uneven participation:

- *Make space for quiet students.* In a whole-class setting, you might extend a general invitation to those who have not yet spoken: "Let's hear from someone who hasn't spoken yet," or "We haven't heard from this table yet." You might also consider extending a specific invitation to particular students; however, we would suggest doing so only if you are certain that they really have something they want to share and just need a little encouragement. It should be okay for anyone to say, "Nothing to say right now." This is an important norm for maintaining a safe environment.

- **Add time.** Sometimes quiet participants just need a little more time to formulate their thoughts. In a whole-group setting, as you introduce each step of the protocol, ask the entire group to pause for half a minute to jot down responses to that prompt. If you think some additional "think out loud" time might be helpful, add a Turn & Talk activity (Chapter 3) after this quiet pause. Then invite students to share comments in the whole group.

- **Use a Go-Round.** Sometimes quieter students aren't sure where or how to enter the discussion. In this case, a simple All-Purpose Go-Round (Chapter 3) can help. (Let students know that they can "pass" when their turn comes, if they like.) Alternatively, as each student speaks, you might have that student call on the next speaker, making sure that it is someone who has not yet contributed to the discussion.

- **Stand by.** If you notice a small-group discussion being dominated by just a few people, go over and stand near the group. Sometimes your physical presence is enough to remind the group to adhere to the "share the air" norm (Chapter 2). If a nonverbal hint is insufficient, you might intervene more explicitly, for example, by saying, "Raise your hand if you have spoken in the last 5 minutes" and then reminding the group that one of the goals is to hear more voices. You can also use the debrief to ask about whether, from the students' point of view, participation was equitable and inclusive.

- **Use speaking cards.** In either a whole-class setting or a small group, pass out several playing cards or plastic chips to each student (try an amount equal to or twice the number of steps in the protocol). Whenever students speak during the protocol, they must give up a chip or a card. When a student has used up all her cards or chips, she needs to remain silent until the debrief step.

CHALLENGE: NO ONE IS TALKING

Although teachers who have never engaged their students in protocols before often worry that no one will speak, this situation is relatively rare. Usually, a thoughtful introduction of the protocol's purpose and the clarity of the structure are enough to ensure at least some participation. If you do run into this situation, consider two possibilities: You may not be not using enough "wait time," or students may not yet be ready for the protocol.

Wait time is the amount of time a teacher allows for silence before speaking. This can happen after the teacher asks a question or between student comments. The research on the use of wait time is consistent and clear: A few seconds of quiet following a question that a teacher poses to the class feels to the teacher like minutes. You might try a couple of strategies for checking to make sure that you are giving students a chance to respond.

- **Reassure students that silence is fine.** You might help students (and yourself) be more comfortable with quiet simply by acknowledging that it happens sometimes: "Protocols are about helping us think together, and sometimes people need quiet in order to think." You can also acknowledge that sitting in silence can be uncomfortable, but everyone will get used to it in time.
- **Use a timer.** Stand where you can keep your eye on a clock or a timer that shows you the seconds that have elapsed. Try to allow a full 30 seconds to go by before you make your next intervention.
- **Write first.** Invite students to write notes for themselves before anyone speaks.

Sometimes, students may not be ready to take on a full-fledged protocol. This may have to do with the unfamiliarity of the protocol structure, the complexity of a protocol, students' current skill level, or the group's current working dynamic. If you begin a protocol and then discover that students are in over their heads, you might try simply acknowledging that for the class in a nonjudgmental way, for example: "Protocols use particular kinds of skills that we don't use every day. Perhaps we should practice those skills a bit and then try this protocol again at a later point." Here are ideas for helping students get ready to use protocols:

- **Try a protocol-friendly activity.** Chapter 3 includes several brief, flexible activities that give students practice in the skills and habits protocols require, for example, Turn & Talk, Warm & Cool, and 3-2-1.

- *Practice one step.* You might isolate a single step of the protocol that you would like to use and have students practice it—then reflect together on how well they did and what they need to improve. For example, students could practice asking clarifying questions (a step in several protocols) or developing warm and cool feedback (key to the Tuning Protocol, Chapter 14). This could be done as a fishbowl discussion, with some students engaged in discussion and some observing (Chapter 18).

CHALLENGE:
STICKING WITH A SPECIFIC STEP OF THE PROTOCOL

Discussion habits are strong and deeply ingrained, even in young students. For this reason, learning to stick to a protocol can be a major challenge. Here are some things that might help.

- *Use sentence stems.* For protocols that provide students with specific prompts, frame those prompts as sentence stems that students need to complete. For example, the second step in the Ladder of Feedback (Chapter 13) is asking clarifying questions. You might ask students to begin all of their contributions during that step with "Could you please clarify _____?"
- *Appoint minders.* In a large-group discussion that you are facilitating, appoint a team of "protocol minders." (Students inevitably come to nickname this role the "protocol police"— ah, well!). The job of this team is to pay careful attention to whether the group is focused on the step at hand and, if they hear people straying, to ring a small bell or give another signal to alert the group. This is a good strategy to use once or twice in learning a protocol, but probably not one you would use as a regular component of the protocol.
- *Pause and write.* After you introduce each step of the protocol, pause to give students a moment to write down their responses and contributions for that step. Encourage them to refer to their notes if the discussion begins to veer off course.

CHALLENGE:
OFFERING FEEDBACK IN A RESPECTFUL WAY

In some protocols, students offer feedback to their peers, for example, the Ladder of Feedback (Chapter 13), the Tuning Protocol (Chapter 14), and some versions of the Gallery Walk (Chapter 12). If your class is not already experienced at giving this kind of feedback, you may need to spend time up front discussing the qualities of effective feedback. Here are some things to try.

- *Share criteria for feedback.* Ron Berger of EL Education (see Resources) offers these criteria to students as they give peer feedback: The feedback must be *specific, kind,* and *helpful.* Have a conversation with students about what each of those words means and what comments that meet those criteria would sound like. Teachers sometimes emphasize the need for students to give "substantive" feedback. Again, have an explicit discussion with students about what that term means and what it looks like in practice.
- *Discuss respect.* Similarly, the term "respect" often needs discussion prior to engaging in a protocol with students: What do respectful comments sound like? In their experience, what kinds of comments feel respectful and disrespectful or unhelpful?
- *Talk about tone.* Tone can be hard for students (or adults) to gauge. Sometimes the exact same comment made in different tones of voice can take on entirely different meanings. You might try setting up some role-plays in which students try using different tones of voice in a discussion.
- *Give feedback on the feedback.* Help students practice how to respond when they feel that they have received unhelpful or disrespectful comments. One way to do this is to encourage students to use "I" statements, for example, "I am a bit confused about . . ." or "I need to know more about . . ."

CHALLENGE:
FEEDBACK IS NOT VERY SUBSTANTIVE

When students first begin giving feedback to one another about their work, their feedback can sound vague: "That was great!" "I think it was okay." "This isn't very good." Here are some strategies for getting students to be more specific.

- *Point it out.* Tell students that, as they offer each piece of feedback, they need to point (literally) to a specific place in the work (text, student work, etc.) that led them to offer the feedback and explain the connection to the group.
- *Get specific.* Before the protocol, have a conversation with students about what vague feedback sounds like and what more specific and substantive feedback sounds like. Capture some sentence stems on the board or chart paper that make it clear what substantive feedback sounds like: "I liked it when you did _____ because _____." Or, "I was concerned when I saw _____ because _____."
- *Use WMYST? cards.* Print a bunch of slips of paper or cards with "What makes you say that?" (or just WMYST?) written on them and give one to each student. Tell the students, "Whenever you hear a piece of feedback that you think isn't substantive enough, hold up this card so that the person who contributed that comment can see it. Then give that person the opportunity to make her comment more specific." (The WMYST cards can be held up by anyone in the group, not just the person who is receiving the feedback.)

The techniques in this chapter are useful not only for protocols but for a wide range of practices for supporting students' learning. In the following chapter, we describe some of these other practices and how they relate to protocols.

CHAPTER 18

Relating Protocols
to Other Practices

A protocol, as a classroom tool, resembles other kinds of tools and techniques to support collaborative learning and thoughtful discussions in the classroom. In this chapter, we review six of these practices: Accountable Talk, fishbowls, jigsaws, restorative practices, Socratic seminars, and thinking routines. For each, we consider the ways in which they are similar to and different from protocols. (For more about each of these practices, see Resources.)

All of these approaches can be useful for supporting deeper student learning and more thoughtful peer collaboration. Protocols, like all educational techniques, are powerful in the appropriate context, but they are not the answer to every puzzle about how to support student learning. They are an important—but by no means the only—tool in the teacher's tool belt. Our purpose in considering protocols in relation to other practices is not to argue for the superiority of protocols but simply to illuminate some of the subtler differences and similarities, in the spirit of supporting teachers in making thoughtful decisions about which techniques to use and when to use them.

Protocols can often be used in conjunction with each of the practices described here. For example, practicing Accountable Talk in the classroom helps students participate more effectively in protocols that involve sharing perspectives with others and responding to and building upon classmates' perspectives, respectfully and productively. The fishbowl can be a way for the class to practice a new protocol or one step of a protocol that has been challenging for them (see Chapter 17). By the same token, the practice students get in protocols that emphasize listening to others' perspectives without judgment (or interruption) prepares them for restorative practice activities.

ACCOUNTABLE TALK

Accountable Talk, developed by the Institute for Learning at the University of Pittsburgh (Lauren Resnick, founder and co-director), is a technique that supports students in developing and using their knowledge by taking part in discussions that are academically rigorous. In classrooms that use Accountable Talk, the emphasis is on helping students to be accurate in their use of facts and rigorous in how they reason with those facts. Students develop these specific skills through evaluating, building on, and questioning one another's ideas.

Students are often provided with sentence starters that help them to substantiate their thoughts (for example, "Based on my evidence, I think _____ "); relate their ideas to the ideas of others (for example, "I agree with _____ because _____"); and critically analyze others' contributions through questioning (for example, "What evidence do you have to support that?"). Accountable Talk can be used in conjunction with a variety of activity formats. For example, in a teacher-guided whole-group discussion, you might ask all students in the class to look for evidence that supports an idea. In small-group discussions, students might work on their own to respond to and develop their ideas, sometimes with the help of prompt cards that remind them of the kinds of contributions and questions that generate a rigorous, academic discussion.

How Is It Similar?

Accountable Talk and protocols share several features: Both focus on supporting the quality of the learning discussion among students, and both are purpose-driven. Whether using Accountable Talk or a particular protocol, the teacher carefully considers the goals of the lesson or the unit and then incorporates selected Accountable Talk prompts or a specific protocol in ways that are most likely to support those goals. Both approaches, along with thinking routines (see section that follows), scaffold specific kinds of thinking for students, whether this is asking clarifying questions in a protocol or building upon a classmate's observation in Accountable Talk. In addition, both rely on repetition to help students build critical cognitive skills and habits of mind. Students need to use the Accountable Talk prompts or the protocol multiple times, with opportunities afterward to reflect on how to improve their effectiveness the next time. Both Accountable

Talk and protocols help students develop important, productive, and transferrable habits of thinking and collaboration.

How Is It Different?

Protocols serve a broader range of purposes than Accountable Talk, which focuses exclusively on helping students develop accurate factual knowledge and rigorous thinking. Protocols might also be used to support careful, analytical thinking, but (depending on the protocol) can also support other purposes: providing feedback to a peer, entering a text, reflecting on one's own preferences and expectations for working on a new project, etc.

Protocols are generally more structured than are typical uses of Accountable Talk. Protocols provide a sequence of specific steps that designate who speaks when and what kinds of things can be said at any given point during the protocol. Because they are highly structured, protocols also tend to place a bit more emphasis on group dynamics. By artificially interrupting the habitual (and often unconscious) flow of discussion, protocols push participants at each step to reflect carefully not only on what they are contributing to the group's work but how they are contributing to it.

THE FISHBOWL

The fishbowl or "fishbowl dialogue" is a strategy for managing a discussion in a large group. The strategy has its roots in the psychological experiments studying group dynamics in the 1960s and 1970s, in which groups were divided into subgroups so that one subgroup could observe the others' interactions. Since then, it has evolved into a popular tool used in education, social work, corporate work, and other settings. To set up a fishbowl, chairs are arranged in a circle in the center of the room. The number of chairs in the fishbowl can vary—anywhere from four or five to half of the total group present. The teacher (or student facilitator) either designates students to sit in the fishbowl or invites volunteers. The remaining students become the observers, sitting or standing around the circle of chairs, watching what goes on inside the "fishbowl."

In a typical use of the fishbowl, the group in the inner circle is given a topic to discuss (which might relate to a controversial question or to a text the whole group has read). While they discuss the topic, the observers take notes, jotting down comments and questions based on their observations. In one variation of the fishbowl, an empty chair is included in the inner circle, and observers are encouraged to sit in it when they have something they would like to contribute to the discussion. In another variation, members of the observing group can tap the shoulder of anyone in the fishbowl, at which point the person in the fishbowl gets up, gives her seat to the observer who tapped her shoulder, and switches to an observer role.

How Is It Similar?

Teachers use fishbowls, as they do protocols, to encourage diverse perspectives on a complex topic. Both can be effective tools for managing a productive, learning-focused dialogue, especially in a large group. The fishbowl technique and most protocols also designate specific roles that participants play, and both can help to heighten participants' awareness about how they are engaging with the group.

How Is It Different?

The fishbowl, strictly speaking, is a tool for organizing the arrangement of the space and the division of roles among participants ("fishbowl participants" and "observers"). It does not specify what the group should talk about or how they should talk about it. Protocols, by contrast, are highly structured and direct the group to talk in specific ways at particular times. Also, unlike fishbowls, which typically involve the entire class as either "fishes" in the center or observers on the outside, protocols can be done simultaneously in small groups.

THE JIGSAW

The jigsaw technique is a strategy for engaging students in cooperative learning. Developed in the early 1970s by Elliot Aronson at the University of Texas and the University of California, the original technique was designed to help mitigate racial tensions among students in the newly integrated Austin Public Schools. It has since been used in classrooms all over the world to give students a way to learn from and with one another.

While there are number of variations, a typical one goes like this: The teacher divides the class into four to six groups and divides the content of the day's lesson into four to six subtopics. (For example, if the class is studying the biography of an historical figure, some possible subtopics might include early life, early career, later achievements, and historical legacy.) One student in each group is assigned to learn about one of the subtopics (often by reading materials the teacher has prepared ahead of time). The students then form temporary "expert groups." For example, all the students who focused on subtopic 1 form a group to discuss what they read about the historical figure's early life, what they think the main points are, and what things need to be shared with their original group. Students then rejoin their original group, and each member of the group takes a turn sharing with the others what she learned about her subtopic. The exercise often concludes with an assessment of students' mastery of the content.

How Is It Similar?

Like Accountable Talk, thinking routines, and protocols, the jigsaw is based on the premise that students can learn more and more deeply through thoughtful discussion with peers. The roles in both the jigsaw and the protocol are clear: In the jigsaw, each person has expertise in or a perspective on the content to contribute to the discussion; in a protocol, each person is clear on whether they are a facilitator, a presenter, or a participant. Both techniques move students through a sequence of steps in order to help them reach an end point.

How Is It Different?

The jigsaw technique is usually used to help students master content. While content might also be the focus of a protocol (particularly those in which students respond to texts), protocols can also be used for a variety of learning purposes (such as discussing a dilemma or offering feedback on a student's research question). In addition, the scope that the two techniques provide are very different. The jigsaw (and similar cooperative learning activities) help to organize the kinds of tasks students will do (that is, learning about a topic, sharing information about a topic) and when they will do them. Protocols, by contrast, are almost always aimed at helping a group organize and sequence the specifics of their actual discussion: What kinds of comments will the group focus on first? second? third? When is the right time to ask questions, to offer responses, to generate new ideas? Most often, protocols focus not on the exchange and mastery of information but on sharing multiple perspectives to deepen understanding of a topic.

RESTORATIVE PRACTICES: CLASSROOM CIRCLES

Restorative practices in the classroom grew out of restorative justice—a set of values, beliefs, and practices drawn from those held and practiced in many indigenous communities, as described by Howard Zehr and other scholars and practitioners. Restorative practices aim to build strong, trusting relationships within a community and invite all the members of the community (not just perceived authority figures) to share responsibility for the health and well-being of the group. One of the most recognizable features of restorative practices in schools is the classroom circle. Classroom circles can be used in a variety of ways to strengthen relationships within classes that have committed to restorative practices—for example, as "check-ins" at the beginning of the day or week, as "check-outs" to close the class session, or as an opportunity for students to share affirmations with one another. Classroom circles are also used to address conflicts when they emerge.

In the traditional classroom circle, students sit in a circle so that everyone can see one another. The teacher reminds students in the group of the circle guidelines or norms, such as "speak honestly" and "listen thoughtfully," and then shares the prompt with the students. The teacher than takes a "talking piece" (often a natural object, such as a stone or a feather) and hands it to the student next to her. The student holding the talking piece responds to the prompt and then passes the talking piece to the next student in the circle, who responds, and so on, until the talking piece has made its way around the circle, giving everyone a chance to share their thoughts.

How Is It Similar?

Classroom circles in the context restorative practices have several features in common with the use of protocols: the importance of the group's arrangement in a physical circle, a focus on equity and enabling every voice to be heard, the goal of surfacing multiple perspectives, and the emphasis on slowing down and listening carefully. Classroom circles and protocols both aim to cultivate skills and habits that students carry with them beyond the immediate circle or protocol.

How Is It Different?

To be effective, classroom circles—particularly circles convened to respond to conflicts or disagreements within the group—need to be rooted in a deep commitment to foundational values and beliefs of restorative practices. Classroom circles are just one part of a larger set of practices designed to deepen relationships throughout a school. These practices seek to challenge and change assumptions about whose voices matter, how norms and rules are established, and what the appropriate response is to students whose behavior does not conform to those norms and rules. Protocols, by contrast, can be used relatively easily as one-off activities. Of course, protocol-guided discussions gain power when they are used consistently and when teachers use them to help cultivate and reinforce student agency, responsibility, and reflectiveness.

SOCRATIC SEMINAR

The Socratic seminar reflects the work of University of Chicago philosopher Mortimer Adler and colleagues in the Paideia Group, active in the 1980s. Also known as "Socratic circle" and "Socratic dialogue," it is a facilitated discussion that engages participants in the thoughtful exploration and analysis of a complex text. In a Socratic seminar, the facilitator (the teacher or a student) asks the group open-ended questions (such as "What do you think this text is trying to say?" "Where does that idea come from in the text?" "What else could that mean?"). The goal of the Socratic seminar is not to debate or to arrive at a correct interpretation but rather to understand more deeply the meaning and implications of the text. The discussion, which can last anywhere from 15 minutes to an hour, is typically followed by a whole-group reflection on the quality of the discussion and how it might be improved.

How Is It Similar?

The Socratic seminar shares many features with protocols, particularly those protocols that focus on analysis of texts (for example, Text Rendering Experience, Chapter 9; Save the Last Word for Me, Chapter 10; and Three Levels of Text, Chapter 11). In text-based protocols and the Socratic seminar, the primary goal is deeper understanding through inquiry and analysis (rather than acquisition of information). In both practices, groups need to establish norms at the outset, particularly norms about respecting others' contributions and monitoring the amount of time one speaks. Similarly, these approaches both develop and depend on the capacity of group members to listen to and respond to one another. In both protocols and Socratic seminars, the facilitator's role is crucial. Finally, both conclude with a debrief or a reflection on the process of the discussion.

How Is It Different?

Perhaps the most significant difference lies in the facilitator's role. In a traditional Socratic seminar, the facilitator prepares ahead of time a series of open-ended questions to which she can refer as she leads the discussion. However, these questions are not asked in a fixed sequence. After the initiating question, the facilitator makes moment-to-moment decisions about which question to ask and how to steer the group. Nor are the questions typically shared ahead of time with the group. The ultimate direction of the discussion is the responsibility of the facilitator and may evolve fluidly as the discussion proceeds. In protocol-guided discussions, by contrast, the facilitator is primarily responsible for encouraging other participants' questions, observations, etc. Also, in a protocol, the sequence of steps and prompts is made transparent for all participants at the outset. While the facilitator is responsible for helping the group move through the established steps, the group understands the process from the beginning.

THINKING ROUTINES

Developed by David N. Perkins, Ron Ritchhart, Jessica Ross, Shari Tishman, and colleagues on the Visible Thinking Project at Harvard

Project Zero, a thinking routine is a short, memorable series of steps that supports students in cultivating specific kinds of thinking. For example, See-Think-Wonder invites students to study an object, an image, or a phenomenon and then to 1) describe what they see, 2) offer some inferences based on their descriptions, and 3) generate questions. Such routines can be used as the basis for individual written reflections or as a guide for a whole-class or small-group discussion.

How Are They Similar?

Like protocols, thinking routines need to be chosen carefully to support the key learning goals of the lesson or unit. Thinking routines and protocols both cultivate intellectual skills and habits, and students benefit from repetition, becoming more skillful with the thinking routine or protocol the more they practice with it. Unlike Accountable Talk (which can take place in structured or unstructured discussions), both protocols and thinking routines, in their original forms, are highly structured activities, providing a series of steps through which students move sequentially.

How Are They Different?

To be an effective thinking routine, the series of steps must be short (usually two to four steps), focused on cultivating a specific kind of thinking (for example, finding evidence or making connections to prior knowledge), and useful as a guide for either group discussion or individual reflection. Protocols, on the other hand, are typically longer (typically, five to eight steps). Depending on the protocol, it might or might not focus students on cultivating a specific kind of thinking. Some protocols, such as the Microlab (Chapter 6), simply invite an open response from the students without specifying a particular kind of thinking they employ.

The primary purpose of a protocol is to support a learning discussion for a group, rather than individual reflection (though many protocols involve periods of individual reflection). For this reason, most protocols involve not only steps that indicate what contributions to make but also steps that specify listening carefully to others' thinking, as well as steps that offer opportunities to respond to or build on others' thinking. They also involve specific roles for the participants: facilitator, presenter, and group. To envision the contrast between a thinking routine and a protocol, imagine a student alone in the evening, doing her homework, and struggling with a particularly challenging reading assignment. If she has had the opportunity to practice with several different thinking routines in her classroom, she might well say to herself, "Hmmmm, what thinking routine could I use to help myself out here?" By contrast, sitting alone on the couch, she would be unlikely to ask, "What protocol can I do to help myself with this assignment?" A protocol requires a group.

Of course, teachers can, in effect, turn a thinking routine into a protocol by structuring the group's use of the routine: by assigning roles, specifying who speaks when, inviting students to respond to one another's comments in particular ways, and so on. By the same token, some parts of protocols (for instance, the prompts in Peeling the Onion, Chapter 8) can stand on their own as thinking routines, which students can draw on to support their thinking and learning even when they're not using a formal protocol. So similarities and differences between the two sets of tools are often simply a function of how and when they are used.

A Schoolwide Culture of Discussion, Inquiry, and Reflection

A group of teachers in an urban elementary school meets regularly, using protocols to develop inquiry questions, examine samples of student work from the teachers' classes, and give feedback on each other's instructional practices. One morning, one of the teachers in the group tells his colleagues that his students asked him what he talked about with the other teachers. When he told the students that the teachers were discussing the work students did in his class, the students were intrigued. He explained to the students, "The other teachers and I use protocols to give each other feedback—just like we do here in class when you are giving each other feedback on your projects and assignments." The students were surprised and delighted to discover that they were doing the same kinds of work that their teachers did.

This story illustrates just one of the ways using protocols can connect teachers and students within a school community. In *The Power of Protocols*, Joseph McDonald and his colleagues describe *protocol pedagogy* as a "signature" approach to teaching and learning that "[invites] collegial readings . . . within trustworthy settings, provoking still deeper levels of reflection, as well as collegial learning" (2013, p. 2).

In this book, we build upon the idea of protocol pedagogy, focusing on protocols as an important tool for supporting collaboration, discussion, and inquiry in classrooms. But of course protocols are equally effective in supporting collaboration, discussion, and inquiry among teachers and administrators. Used in faculty meetings, grade-level meetings, professional learning community meetings, and inquiry groups, protocols can help the adults in the building engage in the same kind of deep and reflective learning that protocols offer for students.

By sharing a common set of tools, students, teachers, and administrators together can build the common language, skills, habits, and

values that support a culture of discussion, reflection, and inquiry—
not just in a single classroom or among a small group of teachers, but
in the school community as a whole. What might you see in a school
with such a culture?

- Students selecting protocols, and other activities, to support
  their collaboration with their peers.
- Students acting as facilitators of protocols for their peers, with
  teachers coaching them.
- Students and teachers talking about the habits cultivated
  through using protocols and how these habits support them
  in different contexts to do their best thinking and work (even
  when they're not using a protocol).
- Students and teachers reflecting on, learning from, and
  celebrating the documentation of learning that has emerged
  in protocol-guided discussions, identifying how that learning
  has fed other endeavors in the classrooms and the school, and
  discussing how to build on it.
- Students and adults using protocols to share their work and
  deepen conversations at events for family and community
  members (e.g., a Gallery Walk to celebrate student work on
  Exhibition Night, a Ladder of Feedback to share reflections and
  identify next steps in Parent-Student-Teacher conferences, or a
  Chalk Talk at a schoolwide parent meeting to dig more deeply
  into questions surrounding a new curriculum in the school).
- Teachers and administrators meeting regularly to share
  their own work and their students' work in protocol-guided
  conversations, identifying and pursuing shared questions
  and goals aimed at improving learning for all students in
  the school, and using protocols to productively explore and
  respond to the thorny challenges and dilemmas that are the
  reality of life in schools.

One doesn't need a school-wide commitment to make using a
protocol effective. A protocol can make a difference in just one class
meeting, one teacher team meeting, or one professional development
session. But protocols gain power when used across contexts and over
time. Generating that power takes more than simple repetition, of
course. The key is the quality of the reflection—reflection not just on
the learning (both collaborative and individual) that has emerged from

the protocol-guided conversation, but on the protocol itself and how the group used it to support their efforts to slow down, dig deeply, explore open-mindedly, question thoughtfully, and share ideas and perspectives respectfully.

Here's another sign that protocols are being well-used to support a schoolwide culture of discussion, inquiry, and reflection: Students, teachers, and administrators have thoughtful conversations about when and how to use protocols, when to adapt them or create new ones, and when to set them aside altogether—because everyone understands that the protocol itself is not the point. The point is the collaborative learning, reflecting, and inquiry that protocols support. As skilled users of protocols, students and teachers realize the limits as well as the benefits of the tool.

Using protocols in this way—with a disciplined commitment that supports thoughtful application and adaptation—yields the greatest value, especially for students. By participating in such reflective discussions, students learn not only to use the tool but also to understand it and shape it to serve their own goals. When students engage in these discussions not just with one teacher or in one classroom but throughout the school, they practice habits of mind and develop an orientation toward inquiry and reflection that carries with them into the world.

Resources

Using Protocols in Professional Development and Meetings

The Discussion Book: 50 Great Ways to Get People Talking by Stephen D. Brookfield and Stephen Preskill. San Francisco, CA: Jossey-Bass, 2016.

The Facilitator's Book of Questions: Tools for Looking Together at Student and Teacher Work by David Allen and Tina Blythe. New York, NY: Teachers College Press, 2004.

Looking Together at Student Work, 3rd Edition by Tina Blythe, David Allen, and Barbara S. Powell. New York, NY: Teachers College Press, 2015.

The Power of Protocols: An Educator's Guide for Better Practice, 3rd Edition. Joseph P. McDonald, Nancy Mohr, Alan Dichter, and Elizabeth C. McDonald. New York, NY: Teachers College Press, 2013.

Protocols for Professional Learning by Lois Brown Easton. Alexandria, VA: Association for Supervision & Curriculum Development, 2009.

School Reform Initiative~Protocols: schoolreforminitiative.org/protocols/

Using Protocols in the Classroom

EL Education~Protocols and Strategies: commoncoresuccess.eleducation.org/sites/default/files/curriculum/grades/ela-3/eledappendixprotocolsand resources0616.pdf

EL Education~Protocols Videos: eleducation.org/resources/collections/protocols -in-action-videos

Facing History and Ourselves~Teaching Strategies: www.facinghistory.org/resource-library/teaching-strategies

School Reform Initiative~Protocols for Youth Engagement: schoolreform initiative.org/protocols-for-youth-engagement/

Related Practices (see Chapter 18)

Accountable Talk:

Accountable Talk Sourcebook: For Classroom Conversation That Works by Sarah Michaels, Mary Catherine O'Connor, Megan Williams Hall, and Lauren B. Resnick. Pittsburgh, PA: Institute for Learning, University of Pittsburgh.

Institute for Learning, University of Pittsburgh~Accountable Talk Practices: ifl.pitt.edu/what-we-do-2/accountable-talks/

Fishbowl:

The Use of a Fishbowl Training Facility with Counselor Education Students by Cass Dykeman and Dick Sampson. Eastern Washington University: files.eric. ed.gov/fulltext/ED379578.pdf

Teaching Tolerance~Fishbowl: tolerance.org/classroom-resources/teaching-strategies/community-inquiry/fishbowl

Jigsaw:

Cooperation in the Classroom: The Jigsaw Method, 3rd Edition by Elliott Aronson and Shelley Patnoe. London: Pinter & Martin, 2011.

The Jigsaw Classroom: www.jigsaw.org/

Restorative Practices: Classroom Circles:

The Restorative Practices Handbook for Teachers, Disciplinarians, and Administrators by Bob Costello, Joshua Wachtel, and Ted Wachtel. Bethlehem, PA: International Institute for Restorative Practices, 2013.

The Center for Restorative Process: centerforrestorativeprocess.com/

Socratic Seminar:

The Habit of Thought: From Socratic Seminars to Socratic Practice, 2nd Edition by Michael Strong. Chapel Hill, NC: New View Publications, 1997.

Socratic Circles: Fostering Critical and Creative Thinking in Middle and High School by Matt Copeland. Portland, ME: Stenhouse, 2004.

Edutopia~Building a Culture of Student-Led Discussion: www.edutopia.org/blog/socratic-seminars-culture-student-led-discussion-mary-davenport

Thinking Routines:

Making Thinking Visible: How to Promote Engagement, Understanding, and Independence for All Learners by Ron Ritchhart, Mark Church, and Karen Morrison, San Francisco, CA: Jossey-Bass, 2011.

Harvard Project Zero~The Visible Thinking Project: pz.harvard.edu/projects/visible-thinking

References

Adler, M. J. (1982). *The paideia proposal. An educational manifesto.* New York, NY: Simon & Schuster.

Costa, A. L. (2008). Describing the habits of mind. In A. L. Costa & B. Kallick (Eds.), *Learning and leading with habits of mind: 16 essential characteristics for success* (pp. 15–41). Alexandria, VA: Association for Supervision and Curriculum Development.

Elbow, P., & Belanoff, P. (2000). *Sharing and responding* (3rd ed.). New York, NY: McGraw-Hill.

Hakim, J. (1997). *A history of us* (3rd ed.). New York, NY: Oxford University Press.

McDonald, J. P., Mohr, N., Dichter, A., & McDonald, E. C. (2013). *The power of protocols: An educator's guide to better practice* (3rd ed.). New York, NY: Teachers College Press

Perkins, D. N. (2003). *King Arthur's round table: How collaborative conversations create smart organizations.* San Francisco, CA: Wiley.

Resnick, L. B., Asterhan, C. S. C., & Clarke, S. N. (2015). Talk, learning, and teaching. In L. B. Resnick, C. S. C. Asterhan, & S. N. Clarke (Eds.), *Socializing intelligence through academic talk and dialogue* (pp. 1–12). Washington, DC: American Educational Research Association.

Spencer, E. (1993). *Three ships for Columbus.* Austin, TX: Steck-Vaughn.

Weissglass, J. (1990). Constructivist listening for empowerment and change. *The Educational Forum, 54*(4), 351–370.

Wells, G., & Arauz, R. M. (2006). Dialogue in the classroom. *Journal of the Learning Sciences, 15,* 379–428.

Zehr, H. J. (2005). *Changing lenses: A new focus for crime and justice* (3rd ed.). Scottsdale, PA: Herald Press.

Zinn, H., & Stefoff, R. (2007). *A young people's history of the United States, vol. 1.* New York, NY: Seven Stories Press.

Zwiers, J., & Crawford, M. (2011). *Academic conversations: Classroom talk that fosters critical thinking and content understandings.* Portland, ME: Stenhouse.

Index

About the Authors

David Allen is an associate professor at the College of Staten Island, City University of New York. He has taught English and ESL at the elementary, secondary, college, and adult education levels. He has been a researcher for projects on authentic student assessment and teacher inquiry at the Coalition of Essential Schools, Brown University; Project Zero, Harvard Graduate School of Education; and the National Center for Restructuring Education, Schools, and Teaching, Teachers College, Columbia University. His most recent books are *Facilitating for Learning: Tools for Teacher Groups of All Kinds* (with Tina Blythe), *Teaching as Inquiry* (with Weinbaum, Blythe, Simon, Seidel, and Rubin), and *Powerful Teacher Learning: What the Theatre Arts Teach about Collaboration*.

Tina Blythe is a researcher at Harvard Project Zero, where she also serves as director of learning and outreach. She is a lecturer on education at the Harvard Graduate School of Education. She began her career as a middle and high school teacher in urban public schools. Her work focuses on creating learning experiences that foster deep thinking and understanding for students as well as for educators. She is particularly interested in the collaborative assessment of student and teacher work. She consults regularly for schools and organizations around the world. Her books include *The Facilitator's Book of Questions* (with David Allen), *Looking Together at Student Work, 3rd ed.* (with David Allen and Barbara Powell), and *The Teaching for Understanding Guide*.

Alan Dichter is the director of the CUNY Affinity Team, providing leadership and instructional professional development for 23 secondary New York City public schools. He has worked as a New York City teacher, principal, director of leadership and new school development, and local instructional superintendent for the New York City Department of Education. He worked as a coach and facilitator for the New York City Leadership Academy and served as the director of leadership development for Portland (Oregon) Public Schools. He is the author of numerous articles on leadership and professional development and is co-author of *The Power of Protocols* and *Going Online with Protocols*.

Terra Lynch is a learning specialist in Austin, Texas, where she works with teachers to design curriculum that supports a wide range of learners. She is a professional development consultant for Metro Learning Communities at the New York University Metropolitan Center for Research on Equity and the Transformation of Schools. She regularly facilitates leadership seminars and professional development workshops with teachers at the elementary, middle, and high school levels in New York and Texas. She began her teaching career in the New York City public schools. Terra has contributed to several books, including *Teaching U.S. History: Dialogues Among Social Studies Teachers and Historians* (Turk, Mattson, Epstein, & Cohen, eds.), *The Power of Protocols, 3rd ed.*, and *Facilitating for Learning: Tools for Teacher Groups of All Kinds*.